It's Your Fault!

An Insider's Guide to Learning and Teaching in City Schools

It's Your Fault!

An Insider's Guide to Learning and Teaching in City Schools

REXFORD G. BROWN

Teachers College, Columbia University
New York and London

Published by Teachers College Press, 1234 Amsterdam Avenue, New York, NY
10027

Library of Congress Cataloging-in-Publication Data

Brown, Rexford.
   It's your fault! : an insider's guide to learning and teaching in city
     schools / Rexford G. Brown
     p. cm.
   Includes bibliographical references (p.) and index.
   ISBN 0-8077-4380-1 (cloth : alk. paper) — ISBN 0-8077-4379-8
     (pbk. : alk. paper)
   1. Education, Urban—United States. 2. Teaching—United States
     I. Title
   LC5131.B76 2003
   370'.9173'2—dc21   2003050760

ISBN 0-8077-4379-8 (paper)
ISBN 0-8077-4380-1 (cloth)

Printed on acid-free paper
Manufactured in the United States of America

10 09 08 07 06 05 04 03   8 7 6 5 4 3 2 1

Contents

Preface

Any story I have to tell is inseparable from the stories of countless others:

Of the pale, scrawny 12-year-old, for instance, who lit fires in the alley behind the school because it made him feel better when he was angry and because he wanted to be a fireman someday;

Or the girl who could not remember anything, could not utter complete sentences, could not think abstractly, but could love like few of us will ever love;

And the boy who trembled and sobbed in my office because he knew that once I told his family about his bullying, his father would beat him;

And the girl who had never been out of her neighborhood and was terrified to get on a plane to go to Disneyland with her class-mates—not because she was afraid of flying, but because she was afraid of what her mother would do to keep her from leaving the neighborhood;

And the girl who was so dyslexic she couldn't read without physical pain, yet somehow managed to raise her reading com-prehension scores eight grade levels in 3 years, and none of us knows how she did it;

And the loudest boy in the world, who was diagnosed as a "counter-phobic learner," someone who won't learn anything because it's more important for him to believe that he already knows it;

And the sweet, slow kid, anxious to please, who watched his brother get shot to death and is now in jail for assault with a dead-ly weapon;

And the girl who would rather be a boy;

And the boy who would rather be a girl.

Any story I might tell is intertwined with the story of the boy who was hauled out of school in handcuffs because he stole things to support his parents' drug habits and then came back to school 2 years later to graduate when he was 20; and his girlfriend, who brought him back into civil society with her love and earned a full-ride scholarship to college;

And the girl whose relatives will behead your dog as a sign that you have offended them;

And the little sniveller who became a bully who became a street kid who became a tagger and now wants to be a graphic artist;

And the boy who started out as the straightest kid in school and became the kinkiest.

Any story I might tell is inseparable from the story of the schizophrenic who came to our school planning meetings and gave us great ideas about how we could communicate more effectively, and the teacher who had a nervous breakdown and left the school and the teacher who had a nervous breakdown, yet kept teaching day after day;

And the teacher who was accused of "inappropriate touching" and the teacher who was accused of racism and the teacher who had her new car "keyed" in the parking lot and the teacher who was called something so disgusting that none of us knew what it meant;

And the teachers who worked two jobs and the teachers who needed summer jobs and the teachers who had to borrow against next month's check and the teachers who left teaching so they could make some money;

And the teachers who wept at staff meetings and the teachers who whooped it up at staff meetings and the teachers who held hands around the staff table and vowed to share their energy and love.

And what about the fathers and mothers and grandfathers and grandmothers and aunts and uncles? The father, for instance, who broke down and told me he knew his son was a sociopath and was going to be a dangerous man someday and nothing could be done;

And the mother who carried her 30-pound, quadriplegic, mute son into my office and told me she wanted to enroll him in my school and when I asked why, said, "Because he's behind in math";

And the father who came to his daughter's suspension hearing wearing a hat that said "Party Till You Puke" and told me that what his daughter needed most was a good thrashing;

And the family that drove 20 miles each way everyday to make sure the kids were safe and in the right school;

And the countless single mothers of 12-year-old boys who told me that something mysterious and awful was happening to their relationship with their sons;

And the countless 12-year-old boys who told me that their mothers were starting to really bug them;

And the parents so victimized by hate that they have become haters themselves;

And the parents blessed with so much love and faith that they cancel out the haters;

And the parents who blame everything on their kids;

And the parents who blame everything on the school;

And the parents who blame everything on themselves;

And the parents who want their children to grow up to be better than them;

And the parents who want their children to grow up to be just exactly like them;

And the parents who don't want their children to grow up at all;

And the parents who told me, "My children never lie!"

And the parents who told me, "Don't believe anything my daughter tells you!"

And the father who called me up crying in the middle of the night and said he didn't know where his daughter was;

And the countless fathers who never called me, who are just not there at all, who appear never to have been there at all;

And the tired, arthritic grandmothers and grandfathers bringing up their children's children's children;

And the hypervigilant parents of anxious, birdlike children who've been classified as "extremely gifted";

And the parents who told me they wanted their children in my school because "no teacher has ever understood my child"; and then returned to my office 3 months later to tell me that none of my teachers understood their child;

And the parents who are terrified that their 6th grader has already lost the chance to get into an Ivy League college;

And the parents who desperately want their children to be both "special" and "normal," treated differently and treated the same as everyone else; whose lives were transformed forever by a genetic mistake, or the jerk of a steering wheel or an innocent fall that snapped a spine;

And the multitudes—*Lo, the multitudes!*—of parents who shop for the best schools and the best teachers year after year; who lavish their love upon their children and will do anything for them, anything; who will fight for them day after day, for as long as they have breath and as long as their sons and daughters can bear it.

Acknowledgments

I am deeply grateful to the Rockefeller Foundation for offering me a residency at the Bellagio, Italy, Study and Conference Center so that I could begin this book. My fellow Fellows there were inspirational and insightful critics, and Gianna Celli and her staff created the perfect environment for thoughtful work. I am grateful to the U.S. Department of Education's National Study of the Uses of Time for the opportunity to learn so much about how time is used in American, European, and Japanese schools and to use that knowledge in writing the chapter "Serving Time." I owe a great debt of gratitude to the students, families, teachers, board members and volunteers who created—and are still creating—P.S. 1 Charter School in Denver, Colorado. From the days when we were only dreaming together, through the tumultuous and wonderful startup years in the old V.F.W. Hall, through our move to our splendid renovated warehouse, and up to the present day, they have been a constant source of inspiration. Particular thanks must go to Mike Green, Marilyn Green, Agnes Sonnenfeld, Mark Ogle, and Tom and Anne Patton for sharing their families' experiences with Special Education.

My greatest debt is to my wife, Sharon, for whose love, wise counsel, and boundless support I will be eternally grateful.

CHAPTER 1

Annie

1

Annie Green has straw-colored hair, bright blue eyes and a dimple in her right cheek. Her mouth is slightly angled toward a half-squinting left eye so that she always appears about to say, "Eh?" In 1995, on the day P.S. 1 Charter School opened, she was 13 years old. Her speech was muddied and she tended to get stuck at the beginning of sentences, repeating her opening words five or ten or more times before moving on to the next part of her thought. I remember when she raised her hand during our first advisement group discussion about what kind of culture we wanted to create in our new school. She said, "I think . . . I think . . . I think . . . I think . . . I think . . . ," her eyes gleaming with urgency, her stubby-fingered hands gesturing, palms up, as if to coax the words out, "Right here . . . right here . . . right here . . . right here . . . , it's right here what you say. It's right here." She smiled a crooked smile, looking around at her classmates, and then sat down.

No one said anything. I thanked her and the discussion moved on. Some students talked about the need for mutual respect, others said kids should rule the school. A few minutes later, she raised her hand again. "Right here . . . right here . . . right here . . . right here . . . ," she began, the same urgency, or perhaps it was passion, the same palm-up gesturing, "Right here it's what you say. It's the kids."

"Right," said another student. "It's up to us." Annie gleamed. She was in a conversation.

On the discussion went, different students contributing their opinions, energy building, and pretty soon there was Annie's hand up again. Again I called on her. "It's right here," she said, "right here . . . right here . . . right here . . . the kids." She looked around for understanding. I thanked her again, and moved on, watching the other students. Two boys were clearly irritated by her long, repetitive preambles. Many looked curious, wondering, it turned out, what was wrong with her.

I already knew what was "wrong" with her, because I had met her and her parents earlier in the summer to talk about whether our program was going to meet her needs. But I hadn't ever had her in a class and I was beginning to wonder if I should always call on her when she raised her hand or if I should skip her in order to keep the class' momentum going. The next time she raised her hand, I ignored her. I called on other students. But she persisted. I skipped her again, because the kids were getting some good ideas out, and I didn't want the energy to drop as we all waited for Annie to say what we now already knew she was going to say. So I called on Angelina, who was clearly a leader and had been making very insightful comments, and she said, "You skipped Annie."

So I called on Annie and she rose and said, "It's right here . . . it's right here . . . right here . . . ," and the two boys started to look impatient and irritated, and then she looked too long at someone and lost her way and then began again, "It's right here . . . right here is the thing, the thing is right here in front."

And someone said, "That's right, Annie."

And I said, "In front of what?"

And Annie said, with a "Harrumph" tone, "Front of our faces!"

She was right, of course, although I didn't know then whether Annie really knew what she was doing when she parroted one of her stock phrases or whether the rest of us were reading things into her words. It didn't make any difference whether she knew what she was doing, though, because she brought all of us to the heart of the matter. It was in front of our faces. It was Annie. Unless and until we—as students and as teachers—could address the troubling fact of Annie in our midst, our discussions about the kind of school culture we wanted would be hollow.

A half-hour into the first day of the first year of our "learning community," and I was already skipping over her and wishing she would let the rest of us have our conversation in peace. But we had vowed that P.S. 1 would be a "full-inclusion" school. I had taken Annie on as my advisee and slotted her into the schedule along with every other middle school and high school student. I knew she was "developmentally delayed"; I knew she couldn't read or write or do math or think about abstract ideas. I knew she had this parrot-like speaking problem and poor articulation, and that she moved awkwardly, and lost confidence in her walking in the dark and on inclines. But three factors had led me to decide to bring her into the founding class of students: First, I was totally smitten by her as soon as I met her; second, I was bowled over by her parents; and third, I and her parents had serious doubts about how Special Education was being practiced in regular schools, and we wanted to find something better. Annie was there to show us the way.

2

Special Education (SPED) began its current life in 1975 as Public Law 94-142, The Education for All Handicapped Children Act, which eventually became the Individuals with Disabilities Education Act (IDEA). It was the culmination of decades of political struggle by parents and teachers of handicapped children to secure rights for a class of people who were being denied, in their view, equal educational opportunity and equal protection under the law. Just as minorities had been systematically denied access to the best schools and the best teachers and the best programs, advocates for the handicapped argued that disabled students were systematically denied access to the learning opportunities enjoyed by more fortunate children. The disabled were in segregated situations as surely as were Black Americans. Their separate and unequal classrooms and schools were, advocates argued, racially biased, instructionally ineffective, and socially and psychologically damaging. PL 94-142 was intended to solve those problems. Under the law, students identified as having cognitive, physical, or emotional disabilities must be given individualized education plans (IEPs) and whatever medical, therapeutic, or rehabilitative services necessary to secure their right to the same learning opportunities afforded everyone else in public schools. Whenever possible, such students also must be placed in the "least restrictive environment" for learning, the ideal being a typical classroom. Over the years, this came to be known as "mainstreaming." Finally, the law extended parents' rights to review teachers' educational decisions about their children and receive due process in any dispute about those decisions.

The number of potential disabilities that might make a student eligible for SPED services started large and grew much larger over the years. A child might be visually impaired or hearing impaired in many ways and to varying degrees. A child might have any of a number of communication disorders—inability to understand, inability to speak clearly, stuttering problems, rushed speech. A child might have physical or health impairments, such as asthma, epilepsy, muscular dystrophy, cerebral palsy, a chronic illness, or a crippling condition of some kind. Students might be identified as having learning disorders, such as dyslexia of various kinds, attention deficit disorders of varying severity, mild to severe retardation, memory disorders, or impulsivity. Potential behavioral or emotional disorders are numerous: temper tantrums, inability to tolerate frustration, moodiness, withdrawal, inability to make or keep friends, fearfulness, anxiety, dysfunctional interpersonal skills, inappropriate feelings, aggressiveness, rudeness, attention seeking, or antisocial behavior. All must be diagnosed and treated. Diagnosis involves creating a social history of the child and his or her family, conducting physical and neurological examinations, doing a psychological workup, testing hearing, vision, speech, and language, and testing cognitive and academic skill levels. Every diagnosis involves a host of service professionals from different disciplines and enormous amounts of documentation, lest there be any questions later on about the process or the conclusions.

SPED has been the single most expensive education reform in history and the single greatest contributor to the rising costs of education over the past 25 years. Although good data are scarce, it appears that we have spent over $800 billion since 1975 (Chambers, Parrish, & Lieberman, 2001; Finn, Rotherham, & Hokanson, 2001; Kakalik, Furry, Thomas, & Carney, 1981). Indirect and ancillary costs could bring the figure to over a trillion dollars. SPED students cost more than twice as much to educate, on average, as regular students—about $13,000 a year per student, and somewhere between $35-60 billion a year, nationally (Finn et al., 2001). The costs have been borne not just by the federal government that mandated SPED (about 12%), but by state governments (56%) and by the districts (32%) that have had to implement the law and have been told by the courts that lack of funds is no excuse for not providing the required services (Horn & Tynan, 2001).

IDEA also has spawned countless national, state, and local associations and organizations, curriculum materials, periodicals for parents and professionals, professional texts, university programs, training seminars, testing and diagnostic materials, lawsuits, and further legislation. Just to give you a flavor, *The Complete Learning Disabilities Directory* (Mars-Proietti, 2002) lists organizations such as the Disability Rights Education and Defense Fund, the National Center for Law and Learning Disabilities, the Attention Deficit Disorder Association, the Council for Learning Disabilities, the Federation for Children with Special Needs, the Learning Disabilities Association of America, the National Association of Developmental Disabilities Council, the National Parent Network on Disabilities, and the World Institute on Disability. Among countless publications, the directory lists *A Parent's Guide to Attention Deficit Disorders, An Introduction to Your Child Who Has Hyperkinesis, Description of Youngsters with Organization/Output Difficulties, Eukee the Jumpy Jumpy Elephant, Shelly, the Hyperactive Turtle,* and *The Parents' Hyperactivity Handbook: Helping the Fidgety Child.* In the legal area are books and pamphlets such as *Legal Rights of Persons with Disabilities: An Analysis of Federal Law, So You're Going to a Hearing: Preparing for Public Law 94-142,* and *Special Law for Special People.* For worried parents, there are such books as *How to Get Services by Being Assertive, Difficult Child, Impossible Child, Misunderstood Child, Living with the Active Alert Child, Raising Your Spirited Child,* and *Solving the Puzzle of Your Hard-to-Raise Child.*

The impact of IDEA on teachers has been profound. For starters, a teacher these days no longer can look at a class of students without thinking of their actual or potential learning disorders. In a class of 30 inner-city students, you might have one or two visually impaired, one hearing impaired, three dyslexics, three ADDs, two ADHDs, three mild-to-moderate behavioral disorders, and 16 "normal" students, some of whom may have undiagnosed problems. Whether it is truly a more diverse group of learners than it used to be, the classroom *seems* more diverse, because you are so conscious of all the actual and potential learning disorders and all the many potential "learning styles" you somehow must address in your instructional planning. And you must fight to discover and focus on their learning *strengths*, because you know so much about their learning *disorders*.

Students with emotional disorders must be treated quite differently than they used to be. You cannot just send them to the principal when they act out, you cannot discipline them the same way you discipline others, you have to tolerate behavior you never used to tolerate, and you cannot suspend or expel them very easily, even when they are violent. Although they do not have the right to disrupt your classroom or to interfere in the learning of others, the fact is that they do both from time to time and you feel compelled to tolerate more of it than you would like because the alternative is going to cost you more time and paperwork.

In response to the knowledge that teachers are facing wider variability in the classroom, teacher trainers and educators give them more and more advice, much of it contradictory. You are told, of course, to *plan*—that is, set goals for the class and the special students, set objectives for the goals, create lesson plans and develop backup lesson plans in case the first ones don't work, and then go into the classroom and *implement those plans*. But you're also told to be spontaneous and flexible, looking always for the "teachable moment" for each child. You are told to keep every student "on task"—but you also are told to encourage divergent thinking. You are told to give students choices—but not too many. You are cautioned not to overwhelm the students with too much material—but you mustn't underchallenge them, either. You are encouraged to make your lessons and materials appropriate to each student's interests, age, developmental stage, and grade level—but it simply cannot be done. Many students are interested in things that cannot reasonably be linked to age or grade level, and, in any case, age and grade level are arbitrary concepts where learning is concerned.

A typical IEP must include very specific information and instructional guidance. It usually includes test results from various batteries, the results expressed in developmental years and months. For instance, the student's age may be 10 years, 3 months, but her reading level is 6 years, 4 months; her mathematical ability is 4 years, 6 months, and so on. There usually will be some description of the student's strengths, followed by descriptions of his "deficits." These tend to be brief and general: "body tone," or "visual motor development," or "auditory processing." IEPs usually contain descriptions of the student's present level of performance, annual goals with respect to each level, short-term objectives, evaluation criteria, dates by which certain skills will be mastered, and specification of instructional strategies, rehabilitative techniques, and materials to be used. Annual goals tend to be general improvement goals: "improve articulation of sounds," or "improve handwriting," or "strengthen fingers of left hand." Objectives, on the other hand, are usually very narrow and concrete: "Terry will pronounce the *t* sound accurately 80% of the time"; "Mary will verbally relay incidents of the previous day every day"; or "John will catch a ball thrown 2–3 feet above his head 75% of the time." Although these files tend to become very thick, special educators usually condense the gist into a page or two for the child's regular classroom teachers. When a teacher finds that one of her students has an IEP, she theoretically can get this short version from the SPED coordinator and use it in her lesson plans. If she is uncertain how to incorporate the IEP into her lessons, she theoretically can get advice from a specialist in "accommodating" special needs students and modifying lesson plans.

As a consequence of IDEA, teachers not only have to face a wider range of student abilities and behaviors than ever, they have to collaborate with a wider range of service professionals than they ever used to—psychologists, social workers, speech and hearing specialists, for instance. They have to create or use a wider range of assessment techniques and instruments. They have to use a wider range of programs and be more knowledgeable about child development. They have to create more lesson plans and learn a wider range of instructional techniques. They have to do more record keeping than ever, in order to document student progress and their own compliance with their students' IEPs. They also have more and different relationships with parents. This is usually good, but it sometimes can turn ugly when a parent insists you do something that you do not think is educationally sound, and the parent has the power to make you do it anyway. Even though these relationships are most often positive, they still require more use of a scarce resource: teacher preparation and time.

3

In this morning I looked in Annie's eyes. My daughter's eyes. I searched for what was wrong. What is her disability? As I looked in her eyes, at her hair blown by night's tossing and turning, she smiled and smiled. My heart hurt with sensations all over. Where is it? I could find no wrong with Annie in her beauty playing with her dog this morning.

Polly danced and barked. Annie sprayed water at Polly's barks. They danced around the room. I felt like I was coming through a thick fog this morning. I cannot see anything wrong with Annie. I cannot feel anywhere in my body that tight almost nauseous feeling I always have when I think I have seen what's wrong with Annie.

In this morning my body feels no tightness, no nausea as I look, and look at Annie. She is simply a beautiful, joy filled child having a morning spraying love and water at her barking dog, Polly.

I set this morning feeling a trembling in my belly. How precious is this moment of me seeing Annie as she is.

So wrote Mike Green, Annie's father, upon having seen what was right with Annie instead of what was "wrong" (Snow & Green, 1994, p. 22). "I finally realized," he wrote later, "that my labeled daughter is not disabled. What disabled her possibility was my belief in disability as her parent. What limited her were the professionals around her believing her to be disabled. She is not dis-abled" (p. 16). Moreover, Mike doesn't believe that *anyone* is dis-abled. In the words of his mentor and collaborator (and Annie's Godmother) Judith Snow, "There are no disabled people. What is real is that there are people who are vulnerable to being stuck in structures that don't support them, or in interactions that lead to stagnant meaning or deepening isolation" (p. 24).

Mike and Judith and Annie's mother Marilyn and, as it turns out, most of the founding parents who came to P.S. 1 with children labeled as SPED students, were, and remain, fervent advocates of a community-oriented, nonprofessional form of "full inclusion." Although their children were entitled to, and had been receiving, SPED services in the public schools, not only were these parents unhappy with the quality of the services, but they were in pro-found disagreement with the underlying *philosophy* of the Individuals with Disabilities Education Act. How can there be an Act for a class of people who do not, in their minds, really exist?

For Mike and Marilyn, the journey to this point of view was a difficult one. For Annie's first year and a half, they had no idea that there was anything "wrong" with her. Neither of them had had much experience with children and, having moved to a new town, they did not have friends with small children. But as Annie approached age 2 and still was neither walking nor expanding her vocabulary beyond baby sounds, the family pediatrician suggest-ed that she might be behind on her developmental milestones and they might want to have her screened. The screening had a twofold impact on Mike. Not only did it reveal that his daughter was, indeed, "developmentally delayed," but it was carried out in a way that triggered what has become a lifelong suspicion of "the medicalized understanding of human beings."

"We went to this meeting after the assessment," he recalls, "and the doctors, the real experts, wouldn't even talk to us. They sent a social worker, who gave us a long list of the things that were wrong with Annie. And in the middle of the meeting, as we're try-ing to absorb all this, I realized that we were being observed through a one-way mirror. I was suddenly furious! I got up and went to the mirror and shouted at whoever was behind it to have the decency to come into the room and sit down with us. I totally lost it. But no one came in. This is how they tell me, essentially, that my daughter is a broken person!"

What both of them remember keenly was the deterministic quality of the diagnosis. Annie was 2 years old. She was "delayed" (a softer word for retarded) and would remain so for the rest of her life. Marilyn refused to believe this. "We just didn't buy it," she recalls. "I developed this theory about how she would grow up. I figured that if she was at 60% capacity now, then when she was 16, she'd be sort of a 10-year-old, and when she was 25, she'd be a 15-year-old, and when she was 40 years old, she'd be all grown up. I kept that fantasy for years, even though I must have known it wouldn't work that way." While Mike's disdain for the experts grew, Marilyn occupied herself with finding someone who might know how to fix her child. Both found themselves becoming "case managers" for Annie.

The first emotional breakthrough Mike remembers came when a man who worked with families of disabled children suggested they go talk to a professor who had done a longitudinal study of children like Annie. "So we went to see this very old— like 300 years old—professor, and he's buried back in the stacks in one of those old medical school buildings—I mean you had to really want to find him to find him—and he had many years ago followed the lives of these children in Boston for 30 years and gone back to find out what was going on with them. And the thing he concluded was that there was no correlation between what the children had been diagnosed and labeled as and what they eventually were doing, 30 years later. So he basically pronounced to us that no one knows what Annie could become. He said, 'The thing you can count on, Mike and Marilyn, is that none of the experts really has any idea what will happen.' That was a wonderful thing to hear. And it was the first experience that kind of demystified this whole medical model for us. We began looking for alternative kinds of things, like family-centered approaches and Waldorf and Montessori preschool environments." Doctors were not the answer.

For a year, Marilyn continued to deny that there was anything seriously wrong with Annie and to dream that Annie would one day suddenly "catch up," that somehow some neurons would connect and she would be normal. She arranged for Annie to attend a preschool for normal children when she turned 3, and has never forgotten the first day. "I took her to the school and within the first 10 minutes I suddenly saw the difference between her and all the other children. It was shocking to see what the other children were like, how much they could do that Annie couldn't. I went home and cried all day." Nevertheless, her dream continued for many years. Somewhere there was an expert who would know the answer or a new program or school that would help Annie catch up.

When she was 4, Annie was chosen for a model evaluation program in speech pathology. It was a nonmedical model that placed a great deal of emphasis on identifying children's strengths and gifts. It worked well with Annie, and Mike and Marilyn were encouraged. When kindergarten came around, Annie entered a public school with a self-contained class for students with severe or profound mental disorders. Annie liked helping the others, but she never left the room to interact with nondisabled students. It was clearly the wrong place for her. Then they tried Montessori, but that didn't work well, either. For first and second grades, they chose a public school known for its "inclusion" policy. What they discovered was that Annie and the other SPED students were isolated in the lunchroom and the music room all day and had no contact with other children. Inclusion apparently meant that SPED students were in the same building as the others. "I couldn't figure it out," Marilyn says. "Annie was supposed to learn how to talk. But she was not around any normal models. How could she learn to talk with people who couldn't talk, either?"

Marilyn began what became years of shopping for the right school for Annie. "I kept asking myself, where does she belong? There has to be *some* place." After several false starts, eventually she heard about Indian Ridge Elementary School in Cherry Creek, whose SPED coordinator wanted to try mainstreaming. Annie was the school's first mainstreamed student, and she remained there for 5 years, under the guidance of Ann Malatchi. Ann was very involved, it turned out, with Judith Snow and the Canadians who were developing alternative approaches to empowering the supposedly disabled. At Indian Ridge, Annie was introduced to the Circle of Friends concept, whereby the disabled person is enabled to do whatever he or she wants to do by joining a community of mutually supportive friends. In addition, Ann Malatchi worked assiduously with teachers to adapt the curriculum to Annie's needs. Annie thrived in this environment.

Unfortunately, Annie had to leave Indian Ridge to go to middle school, and her middle school was not very accommodating. "It was a huge, stressed-out school," Marilyn recalls, "and the teachers were actively hostile to mainstreaming. Annie spent all day in the resource room and had no contact with regular kids." She was teased, too, when she rode the school bus. One day, when Marilyn picked her up at the bus stop, she saw a boy mimicking Annie's talking and walking. "It broke my heart," Marilyn says. "And I decided that night that I would have to talk to Annie about how people were going to make fun of her—because you know how guileless and innocent she is and I didn't want her heart broken, too. So I had the 'differentness' talk with her. I said, 'You know how your friend Jennifer is different?'—thinking of her friend who is in a wheelchair and partly paralyzed and can't talk well. And I thought Annie would say, Yes, she can't walk and she can't talk and so on. But Annie said, 'She's very quiet.' And I realized that Annie doesn't see what people can't do. She doesn't think that way. That was a big lesson for me. I realized again that, yes, Annie's different—but there's nothing *wrong* with Annie."

When Mike heard about P.S. 1 from some friends, he told Marilyn and, as she puts it, "we grabbed onto you-all like a lifeboat! We were so excited! And then Annie, she was the proof that it was the right decision. She's always loved school. But I'd never seen her so excited. She knew she was home from day one. And from then on, she *hated* being away from school. She was furious at me for years because I wouldn't let her go to school on weekends! I finally figured out she thought all the kids were there on Saturdays and Sundays and I was keeping her away, and she was furious at me." Annie fit in because P.S. 1 was wide open to ideas about how to help people learn without labeling them or isolating them from the larger community. Our philosophy was that all learners have strengths and weaknesses, all deserve personal learning plans, all must work at their own paces, and all require a community within which to find support and maximize their gifts.

Mike particularly liked those ideas because he had become, during Annie's childhood years, an increasingly vocal critic not only of the medicalized model of human disabilities, but of the full range of public and privately funded programs that aim to help people but, instead, create dependencies and subvert community solutions to human problems. His radicalization began with his experiences with Annie, which did not sit well with him. He knew there was something wrong with the system that supposedly was designed to help Annie because it felt so dehumanizing and was so disempowering. His search for alternatives that simply *felt* better led him to Judith Snow, a philosopher at the Centre for Integrated Education and Community in Toronto. Judith is a quadriplegic who was supposed to have died from all her physical ailments decades ago but has managed to live a full and productive—in fact, very spunky—life, against all the odds. She maneuvers her wheelchair by blowing or sucking on a tube, types using a breath-operated Morse Code system, and goes wherever she wants whenever she wants, with the help of a Circle of Friends who have even gone so far as to break her out of an institution. Mike met her at a summer institute on integrated education at McGill in 1993 and has been a devoted friend ever since. "Judith personified everything I had dreamed of for Annie, but never thought was possible," Mike recalls. She also wrote persuasively about the bankruptcy of the concept of disability. "The paradigm of disability loads us down with two insupportable choices," she wrote in 1993. "Either we spend endless dollars, time and frustration uselessly attempting to eliminate limitations in each other and getting mad at each other when it doesn't work or we abandon people to attics, isolated SPED rooms, group homes, institutions, poor health, wasted lives and even death itself" (Snow & Green, 1994, p. 16). The better paradigm, she believes, is to conceive of everyone as gifted in some way. Giftedness, to her, is "the possibility of meaningful interaction based on differences in how people are, what they do and what they have" (p. 20). In the disability paradigm, we expend resources to overcome limitations; in the giftedness paradigm, we expend resources to build communities and foster participation in them.

Judith, in turn, led Mike to John McKnight, a professor and director of the Community Studies Program at Northwestern University in Chicago. McKnight, author of *The Careless Society* (1995), has written extensively about the power of authentic democratic communities and the ways in which they are being systematically undercut by professional practices and bureaucratized helping systems. He is deeply concerned about what Rick deLone (1979) once referred to as "help that can hurt"—gigantic service technologies that have turned many Americans into dependent clients and destroyed their capacity to be citizens. He is sharply critical of human service professions that require an apparently endless expansion of human "needs" and "deficiencies" that must be labeled and remedied by experts and government programs. What has happened is that "human service professionals with special expertise, technique, and technology push out the problem-solving knowledge and action of friend, neighbor, citizen and association," he wrote (McKnight, 1989, p. 9). "As the power of profession and service system ascends, the legitimacy, authority, and capacity of citizens and community descend. The *citizen* retreats. The *client* advances" (p. 9, emphasis in original). This was the point of view that Mike Green contributed to P.S. 1 in the months before its opening, and it explains why he was so excited by the school's potential.

Because of Annie, Mike became a social worker and therapist—but one who couldn't trust the system he was working in because of the way it described his daughter. The more he worked with McKnight and Snow, the more he saw that labeled people had to be decategorized and brought into communities as full and valued citizens. Yet his work also revealed a steady erosion of the kinds of natural communities that are necessary to restore fullness of life for both the labeled and the unlabeled. He began to take an interest in "intentional communities," a term coined by McKnight's friend Ivan Illych. "It's so clear that it's hard enough for any of us to feel a sense of community, especially in the inner city—let alone people who have been labeled," Mike says. "We began looking for and thinking about 'intentional communities,' sanctuaries where the deep core value is to welcome people from the edge—not just for the benefit of the people from the edge, but for the benefit of the community as a whole. The community needs *everybody's* gifts in order to be healthy. Illych said they were sort of like medieval monasteries. So then I began asking myself, what is a value-based community that has boundaries around it and has enough strength that, at its core, it would welcome somebody like Annie? And I thought: P.S. 1 is one of those places. It aimed to be hospitable—not in a 'hi, how are you' kind of way, but in a 'it's *necessary* for me to welcome you, because I need you as you need me' kind of way."

What Mike and Marilyn had found out over the years was that the "inclusion" that mainstreaming offered to students like Annie was incomplete. Yes, students who formerly had been excluded from regular classrooms were now in them more often than they had been in the past. But most schools are not communities in even the remotest sense. Students are compelled to be there, have no say in what goes on, and do not engage in fundamental conversations about the common good or their mutual plight. "They're institutions," Mike says. "To the extent that what passes for inclusion works in schools, it's because *all* kids are institutionalized. But the degree to which it results in something real—that is, not Annie participating, but Annie being *invited* to participate—is much more important than just the fact that she's there. And it's not about programming, it's about the community context, the true hospitality." Programming cannot do for a person what genuine acceptance and participation in a natural or intentional community can do: make them able citizens. What the supposedly disabled need most, in Mike's view, is to have their gifts recognized and *understood as necessary for the security and completeness of the rest of us.*

4

Special Education programs alone cannot provide the context necessary for people to see each other as they really are and to participate fully in a democratic civic life. Indeed, they perpetuate the paradigms of disability, professionalism, and clienthood that people like Mike find so destructive to our personal and social health. This was a major reason why we designed P.S. 1 as a "learning community," not a school, and why we were reluctant to have a Special Education program, *per se*. But the critique of SPED is broader even than this, and it cuts to the heart of what's so wrong with our education system in general that people like us wanted to start our own schools. Whatever the good intentions of its advocates, whatever their purity of heart, IDEA is crippled by its legalistic and bureaucratic packaging and by a major disconnection between scientific "diagnoses" and educational "remedies."

The legalistic packaging of SPED weakens it in several ways. To begin with, most of us would prefer to help others out of compassion or an acknowledgment of our mutual interdependence, or out of a civic or religious sense of duty, or because we see that it would be to our advantage to do so. We don't like doing good things because we *have* to or we'll be hauled into court. Legislation that tells educators what they must do under penalty of law gets things off on the wrong foot and creates forms of resistance that would not necessarily be there in different circumstances.

Second, most of us understand that life is more gray than black-and-white and that no law can anticipate all that might happen in our relationships or accommodate all the give and take a situation might require. Laws regarding social problems are necessarily simplistic and reductive and either too vague or too narrow to serve as anything more than rough guides for action. They can establish frameworks for solving complicated human problems, but they are never, in themselves, the solution.

Third, the legal process is necessarily adversarial. Reasonable people with the same love of a child and the same goals for his or her future become adversaries even when they do not want to be. Positive energies are easily transformed into negative energies, insignificant differences are exaggerated to dramatize legal positions, trust necessary for any solution to work is undermined, and valuable time is wasted. Each party focuses on his or her good, but no one focuses on the common good or on larger perspectives beyond the letter of the law within which the dispute might be resolved.

This is especially so with regard to laws that establish rights for a group of people who believe themselves to be victims of some kind of injustice. There are many ways to correct injustices, but in our time, following the example of the civil rights era, we try to correct them by giving groups new rights. Those of us who have lived through that era and fought for those rights have learned that however important it might have been to ensure equal protection under the law and to eliminate discriminatory intent from the law, prejudice, injustice, inequality, and discrimination remain. They are social problems, not legal problems. Legal action, in itself, is always insufficient to solve community problems. Moreover, when you try to describe a social problem in terms of rights, you tend to weaken the very sense of community that may be necessary to ameliorate it. This is because rights are absolute. When I have a right to something, I don't have to bargain for it, or compromise for it, or even listen to what you may think about it. I don't even have to talk to you about it. As Philip Howard (1994) pointed out in *The Death of Common Sense*, once we started down this road, "people armed with new rights could solve their own problems by going straight to court, bypassing the maddeningly slow processes of democracy" (p. 124). The result is what Howard calls "a nation of enemies"—groups of people, each armed with absolute rights, pitted against each other in endless unsatisfying lawsuits.

Particularly troublesome is the legal concept of due process, which is often at issue in rights litigation. It sounds simple—everyone has a right to due process in deliberations or decisions affecting their substantive rights. But what is due process in a specific instance? If a teacher sees that a curriculum is not working for a SPED student and makes some changes on the fly, were the student's parents denied due process? How *much* process is required? How many meetings, how many different people involved in a decision, how many sign-offs from how many supervisory levels? How much judgment can a knowledgeable professional exercise without consulting others? The fact is, due process is indefinable.

There are no legal substitutes for trust, intelligent debate, discretion, and muddling through. It is both impossible and undesirable to try to prevent people from learning the hard way, through trial and error. The more the law attempts to eliminate human error, the more it prevents human learning.

The legalistic framework of the IDEA burdens the spirit of its intentions. Bureaucracy buries the spirit entirely. The American system of education is heavily bureaucratic, partly because it is the most overregulated enterprise in America, partly because it is a monopolistic enterprise, and partly because it carries the genes of the early-twentieth-century, mechanistic organization. Its key values are impossible to actualize well or consistently in the real (i.e., human, messy) world: objectivity, control, uniformity, certainty, and compliance, for example. Its chief means of trying to actualize its values are centralization, rational planning (goals, objectives, subobjectives, schedules, deadlines, etc.), rules, regulations, formal processes, hierarchical management structures, routines, and documentation. These values and means shape every program a bureaucracy administers, regardless of its moral content.

Within the hard outer shell of its mechanistic bureaucracy, the education system has grown a softer professional bureaucracy that does most of the educational work. The people in this core are trying to educate children and young adults. Their loyalties are to the values of their discipline, which exists outside the system, providing its own research-based instructions, professional organizations, and means of achieving esteem. Like their managers, however, education professionals believe in rational, technical problem solving. They believe in specializing, standardizing, and formalizing. Those who are in branches of education with roots in the sciences or social sciences—educational psychologists, counselors, and many kinds of Special Education teachers—are especially prone to think in these ways. They are technocrats, trained to think of themselves as experts, obligated to carry out programmatic imperatives formally, equitably, and efficiently. They develop categories of help, train specialists in those categories, and create programs that will help the greatest number of people for the least expense.

This brings us back to Mike Green's and John McKnight's critique of the medicalized understanding of disability and the "helping professions" that can hurt. By packaging SPED in a professional bureaucracy that is itself embedded in a mechanistic bureaucracy, we once again have undermined the ends of the law with the means of its implementation. IDEA calls for interdisciplinary teams of parents, teachers, and professionals to collaborate in the creation of individualized plans for each child. This would require lots of informal conversations, everyone making adjustments, innovation, a sense of team responsibility, revision when things don't go as planned, and a sense of interdependency—in short, a community of inquirers and interpreters. But this is not what professional and mechanistic bureaucracies encourage. This interdisciplinary, community-oriented model suggests far more subjectivity, discretion, judgment, and undocumented activity than the system can permit. It conflicts with the system's need for an efficient repertoire of diagnostic categories, equitable procedures, standardized programs, measurable goals, and someone in charge who can be held accountable for mistakes and failures. The spirit of IDEA does not fit with the education system's dominant organizational form and its values.

5

The knowledge base for the diagnosis and treatment of physical, cognitive, and behavioral disorders is a mélange of hard science, soft science, quasi science, social science, psychology, and folklore. In each category, major disputes rage about substance and procedure. The knowledge base for teaching and learning is a mixture consisting of a little science, a lot of practical knowledge (or "craft knowledge"), and a goodly amount of its own folklore. This knowledge base, too, is riven with disputes. Between each knowledge base and its practitioners stand schools of education and countless teacher training workshops as vehicles of transmission. Between the more scientifically based diagnostic disciplines and the more humanities-based implementation disciplines lies an ancient gulf in understandings about the nature of knowledge itself and its role in the perfection or destruction of social beings. The more scientifically oriented people working in the field of disabilities do not have a lot of respect for educators. Educators over-respect supposedly scientific knowledge and practice, while underrespecting their own knowledge and practice, to the extent that they understand it at all. Into this "system" wanders the family of the supposedly disabled child: mom and dad filled with guilt, anger, and anxiety; little Billy just wanting some friends to play with.

Diagnosis of disabilities is at least as much art as it is science, for two reasons: Many, if not most, Special Education candidates have more than one problem; and many neurological and psychological disorders overlap or share similar symptoms, even though they entail different treatments. For instance, Annie's strange speech patterns could be related to a central auditory processing disorder (CAPD), a short-term auditory memory deficit, general apraxia (the brain has trouble organizing volitional production of speech), mixed receptive expressive disorder (MRELD), semantic pragmatic disorder (SPD), aspergers, pervasive developmental delay (PDD), severe expressive language disorder (SELD), sensory integration dysfunction (SID), or autism. All of these conditions are related to each other and some are subcategories of others. If she has a form of MRELD, it, too, is related in various ways to Tourette's syndrome, attention deficit hyperactivity disorder (ADHD), obsessive compulsive disorder (OCD), aphasia, or PDD-NOS, a condition characterized by children talking in memorized sentences, but not knowing what they mean. Experts can rule some of these out relatively quickly, but they seldom can rule out all but one, and *they have to be experts*. Moreover, even experts cannot be sure when a particular symptom is a consequence of an underlying organic disorder or of a transient situation. For example, it is reasonable to suppose that, when Annie's parents went through a divorce, she felt the same things other children of divorce feel. Did she exhibit symptoms that were attributed to her underlying condition or to a temporary family condition? If you believed her behavior reflected a permanent organic condition, you would recommend one remedy. If you believed it was a psychological reaction, you would recommend something else.

Although scientists are learning an enormous amount about the brain every day, they still have much to learn about neurological disorders and their specific impact on learning capacities— especially if "learning" is interpreted broadly and not just in terms of "school learning." One of Annie's classmates, Ben, suffered a closed-head injury at age 15 months and came out of his coma with a very grim prognosis. Over the years, his parents, Mark and Agnes, searched in vain for information about how to help him learn. Little was available, because most children with Ben's injury do not survive as long as Ben has survived and adults with traumatic brain injuries acquired them later in life. Diagnostic tests were useless because they were tied to traditional notions of school learning and were developed for people who had never had traumatic head injuries. Another of Annie's classmates, Chris, is autistic. The more science learns about autism, the more forms of autism there appear to be and the less certain parents become of any particular diagnosis.

A number of P.S. 1 students have been diagnosed as "dyslexic." Dyslexia is probably the most well-known category of learning disorder. For much of the past century, dyslexia was thought to be related to intelligence, motivation, or even retardation. As recently as the early 1990s, it was thought that it was a visual problem. For some reason, students' eyes were mixing the letters up and reversing words. The logical inference from this diagnosis was that students should undergo eye-training exercises of various kinds. We now believe that dyslexia is a range of problems students' brains can have in processing language, especially language sounds. Their brains cannot connect the written symbols on the page with specific phonemes. The logical inference from this diagnosis is that students should undergo ear training. In the time it takes for a remedial program to be understood, taught, and implemented widely, research has completely changed our understanding of the underlying mechanism of the disorder.

The point I am making is that it takes sophisticated people who are up on the latest research and have seen a great many children to make accurate diagnoses of learning disorders. The average SPED team does not possess that sophistication, especially if the school is outside a large urban center. Schools are guaranteed to be behind the curve with respect to diagnosing and treating a reading problem that affects the poorest-performing 20% of students to some degree.

Of all the categories of SPED students, the largest is learning disabilities (LD). About half of all SPED students have been identified as having a specific learning disability—a growth of 233% since the mid-1970s. Dyslexia accounts for many of those diagnoses, but the fastest-growing and most controversial categories are ADD and ADHD. Children in these categories don't seem able to pay attention. They don't listen in class. They fidget. They can't sit still. They bother other students. They don't do their work in class and they don't turn in homework. They're impulsive. They forget their assignments; they lose books and papers and worksheets and backpacks and locker locks and bus tokens and lunches and jackets and sweaters and shoes and supplies. No matter how many times you insist on it, they forget to bring pencil or paper to class. Many ADHD children, in addition to these traits, are explosive and inflexible. They misbehave constantly and seem unable to learn from the ensuing punishments or consequences or long, rational discussions about their behavior. Many can't be reasoned with and do not think that what they do is wrong—for instance, hitting other kids. You can go on and on with them about the Golden Rule and their behavior contracts and the law, and they just keep doing what they do. They can be absolutely maddening.

The problem with an ADD or an ADHD diagnosis is that it rests heavily on children's behavior that could be explained by any number of other neurological diagnoses (it has been linked with Tourette's, expressive language disorders, auditory processing disorder, and autism, for instance), or by psychological problems, or by family, social, and institutional dynamics. ADHD almost never appears in a pure form. Edward Hallowell, in his popular book, *Driven to Distraction* (1994), lists 22 conditions that may accompany, resemble, or mask ADD. ADHD cannot be detected by any known neurological or psychological test. To be sure, many of these children change their behavior somewhat under the influence of drugs such as Ritalin, Clonadine, or Depakote. But they also would change their behavior somewhat if we hit them over the head with a two-by-four every morning. Their changed behavior is not necessarily a sign of an organic illness. There is some evidence that ADHD runs in families, but many nonorganic things run in families, too: abuse and neglect, for instance, or early childbirth, or poor nutrition, or neuroses. As with dyslexia, the cluster of behaviors that have become ADHD have been diagnosed and treated in many different ways over the decades. Once, children like these were simply bad seeds, devil children in need of the strap and a good dose of religion. They were just, as my grandmother used to say, "trouble looking for a place to happen."

In the 1950s, we looked at child and adolescent behavior through psychoanalytic lenses that explained rebellion, withdrawal, oppositionality, impulsiveness, argumentativeness, inflexibility, violence, and juvenile delinquency as unsatisfactory attempts to resolve fundamental unconscious conflicts. To the psychoanalytic explanations of difficult children were added various social explanations. Minority students were not doing their work or obeying teachers because they were victims of oppression or because they didn't want to buy into anything White, like the education system. Minority children had different learning styles or were more "high spirited." Their behavior was the fault of an insensitive school system that was designed for White suburban kids.

These social and ethnic explanations of behavior were not just layered on top of psychological models of behavior—they discounted or contradicted them. A common perception of psychological explanations is that the child's behavior is his or her parents' fault. It's bad enough having a child who's driving you crazy. Who wants to take the blame for it, too? Or to have one's culture blamed for it? Minority families, it has been argued strenuously, have their own ways of raising children, which White teachers and social workers do not understand or accept. Single moms have enough burdens to carry. Must they carry guilt for being single, as well? Teen moms were punished enough during their teens; must they be blamed for their children's behavior and their children's children? Middle-class moms and dads do not like to be blamed for their children's behavior, either. So they left their child with sitters and put their careers first; they gave him all the material comforts a boy could want. How dare anyone say they "neglected" him? How dare anyone infer that he is trying to get attention at school because he gets none at home?

Even if there were no organic basis for the behavior of inattentive and hyperactive students, you can see why many people would want to find one. The burdens of moral, psychological, and social disapproval are too much to bear. It would be nice to believe that learning problems were consequences of organic, genetic factors with no relationship to how we love or parent. Some clearly are. Some, like ADHD, have elements of both nature and nurture. I raise this point only to illustrate the perils of diagnosis. I have seen ADHD students who clearly are hard-wired to be the way they are. Something biochemical is going on and has been going on since they were born, and something biochemical may be called for in order to help them learn. I have seen students labeled ADD and ADHD whose behavior is better explained by family and social dynamics. Careful, long-term observation by a sensitive team will sort out the difference, if a family will stay in the same school long enough or if a student's new special educator will communicate with his or her prior special educators. Absent those conditions, however, the potential for misdiagnosis and mistreatment is great. Classroom teachers are left with the job of figuring out how to engage a larger and larger proportion of students who are, for whatever organic and/or psychosocial reasons, unengageable.

The typical recommendations for how to accommodate ADD and ADHD students in the classroom involve giving them lots of "structure." Give them lists of things to do, reminders to do them, previews of what you're going to teach them, repetition of lessons, explicit directions, and frequent feedback on progress, such as daily report cards. Break large tasks into small ones, simplify instructions, and provide detailed schedules and outlines of what they are to do. Set firm limits to their behavior, specify all conceivable rules, and enforce them promptly and consistently. Since their disorder appears to have something to do with cognitive and emotional disinhibition, inhibit them.

This approach seems like a rational remedy, but it is fraught with problems. First of all, it requires an enormous amount of work. Second, no matter how many lists and reminders and schedules you might prepare for a child, his or her parents can always say that you should have prepared more. No one knows how much structure is enough. Third, most of these students are pretty intelligent and imaginative. This kind of "dumbed down" instruction bores them quickly, and it should. Fourth, the virtues of structure sound suspiciously like the virtues of rationalism run amok. We are saying, in effect, that the cure for this condition is to turn the child into a little bureaucrat. Fifth, this approach is flawed because it is mostly about training, not learning. The human brain doesn't learn this way. And finally, it is hard for children not to feel they are being punished somehow. Since so many of them have behavior problems as well as cognitive processing problems, they can be excused for not seeing much difference between explicit punishments for misbehavior and implicit punishments by means of a condescending and demeaning curriculum.

While students with learning disorders account for the largest group of SPED students who have been mainstreamed into classrooms, those labeled with emotional and behavioral disabilities are the next largest group. Students with learning disorders require teachers to be clinical psychologists; students with emotional and behavioral disorders require teachers to be psychiatrists. We once had a student who would blow up at the least provocation, scream "Fuck you!" at the teachers, and run from the school. I called her mother, who told me that her daughter had "oppositional defiant disorder" (ODD). I said I was somewhat oppositional to her daughter behaving like that. She brought her daughter's therapist in to confirm the diagnosis and to give me some constructive things to do when her daughter insulted people. "She doesn't really *mean* 'fuck you,'" the therapist said. "You have to look for the positive intention behind her actions." After some months of looking for positive intentions and finding none, we finally let her go.

Estimates of the proportion of children with ODD range from 7% to 25%. A greatly disproportionate number of them are minorities from poor homes. The diagnostic risk factors ensure that this would be so: low income, low family level of education, teenage pregnancy, isolation, high-stress living environment, single parenthood, parental chronic illness, criminal history in the family, drug abuse, marital discord, physical abuse, low cognitive stimulation, inconsistent parenting, and parental alienation from social institutions like school. Such factors, especially in combination, lead to troubled and difficult kids. Throw in conscious or subconscious racism, classism, and school environments that all but beg any red-blooded student to be defiant, and you have a prescription for daily chaos in countless classrooms.

The choices teachers have for dealing with defiant SPED students are all bad. If they begin acting out, you send them out of the classroom, which means they're not learning anything, which means they fall farther and farther behind their classmates, which means they tend to act out more when they return, because that's all they have left to contribute. If you try to deal with their behavior in class, you are shortchanging the other students. If you just let them carry on, you are again shortchanging the students who want to learn. If you write up everything that happens, as you are supposed to, and have all the conferences you are supposed to have with parents and specialists, that one student is going to cost you an inordinate amount of your time and energy. If the student is a minority, you and others constantly will question whether the defiance was caused by your insensitivity to his cultural norms, your fear of high-spirited minority young men, your insecure need to assert control over your classroom and not lose face in front of your students, or any number of other possible sources of bias in your judgment.

These days, students are very sophisticated about how to exercise their power and keep adult power at bay. Whatever your ethnic heritage or gender, any student can call you a racist or can say you touched him or her "inappropriately." This can lead to anything from minor inconveniences, to suspension (pending an investigation), or to the end of your career, regardless of the merits of the accusation. Students know this and teachers know they know this. A single student with, say, borderline personality disorder, can throw an entire school into enough turmoil to ruin morale for years.

It is sad to see how many young people are suffering from various degrees of depression, anxiety, debilitating anger, panic attacks, eating disorders, abuse trauma, drug addiction, and compulsive self-mutilation. P.S. 1 is a small school, but we have had students with all of these problems and more. It is estimated that as many as 9.5 million young people under the age of 18 suffer from these and other emotional and behavioral afflictions. I believe it. Most are undiagnosed. Teachers know there is something wrong with these students, but they are not trained to either diagnose or treat such problems. Moreover, these are "personal" problems, just over the line most teachers draw between their business and students' business. Yet, when you have a child weeping quietly in the corner, what are you to do?

Diagnosis of learning and emotional disorders is extremely tricky, must be done by experts who are in short supply, and changes rapidly with burgeoning research. Training materials, college courses, and workshops take years to develop and reach only a fraction of the people who need the information. Parents have been known to insist that their child receive an IEP even when she does not need one, reasoning that the risks of stigmatizing their child are offset by the benefits of extra resources and attention. A great many students become eligible for SPED services simply because they are two or more grade levels below their peers on standardized reading tests. Whether or not anyone can find anything actually wrong with the child, it is *assumed* that something must be wrong, or the child would be performing "at grade level." Look hard enough for a disability in any of us, and you will find one. Is it possible that any of these children are behind not because they have learning disabilities but because their schools have teaching disabilities? Has the category of LD mushroomed so dramatically in the 1990s because diagnosis of learning disorders has become so much better or because diagnosis of school complicity in student failure has become so much worse?

Undoubtedly, many SPED students have been diagnosed accurately, at least for the time being. (As they age, the diagnosis may become inaccurate.) The next question is whether anyone really knows what to do *educationally*, as a consequence of a scientific diagnosis. I am skeptical about this, because I have seen so many IEPs that recommend the same educational strategies for very different disorders. This may mean that the education system has caught a lucky break. What a blessing, that dozens of disorders can be remedied with the same curriculum, goals, and objectives! Alternatively, it might mean that educators know only a few learning strategies and instructional techniques, and those are the only remedies available, regardless of the disorder. The individualizing that IEPs call for is happening in the close attention to the child and the discussions about how he or she learns best. But the actual program that results from these sometimes very rich and illuminating discussions is nowhere near as nuanced and thoughtful as the discussions themselves, both because the educational repertoire is so limited and because many of the things one might want to do to help an individual student learn *cannot be done within the framework of the traditional classroom.*

We *may* know what is wrong with the student, although there is a good chance that we are wrong; we *may* develop some interesting ideas about how to help her learn, but our solution repertoire is very limited; and we *may* develop a plan that could be implemented in some ideal classroom, but there is a good chance that it cannot and will not be implemented in a real classroom.

6

Although she could not read, write, or calculate, Annie was in the same classes as anyone else. In my English classes, I would have Annie "write" when everyone else was writing. She would clutch a pencil tightly and write line after line of wiggly semblances of letters, the first line extending the full width of the paper, the second indented to be a little shorter, the third line indented still more, until the last line on the page was an inch long. If a stranger had entered the room, he would have seen no difference between Annie's concentration on the task and other students' concentration. But he would not have been able to read a word of what she wrote.

When the writing was done and discussion began, we would ask Annie to talk about her writing, as all the other students talked about theirs. Usually, she would say, "Writing. My writing." She would look at squiggles and have no more idea what they meant than the rest of us did. Annie did not know that writing was *about* something. It was an act she could imitate, but not understand. If a classmate asked, "Is it about your trip with your dad?" she'd answer, "Yes. My trip! Went to MOTEL!" But if the classmate had asked, "Is it about your dog Sparky?" she would have said, "Yes! Sparky's my dog!" and launched into a disjointed, but highly entertaining, soliloquy about Sparky. It was entertaining because Annie could be very funny and she knew it. She wouldn't just say, "Sparky's my dog," for instance; she'd say, "Sparky's my DAWG," and she'd draw the word out for comic effect, breaking us up every time.

Whatever Annie did not know about why people write, she at least knew that they write in order to talk with one another, and she loved to do that. Whatever linguistic, syntactic, or mechanical skills she lacked, she compensated for with her great sociability. As we teachers slowly adjusted to Annie's presence in our classrooms, we began to see more and more ways in which she contributed to the class. This is very difficult for teachers. We want to *teach*, and we want to teach *something particular*, and we spend enormous amounts of time concocting ways to make our students *learn* those things. Our professional esteem is bound to our success in this endeavor. If students do not or cannot learn what we are trying to teach them, it drives us crazy. It is not our habit to discover learning that we did not plan or to find compensations for failure. It does not make immediate sense to us to have a total illiterate in our literature class or a person in algebra class who cannot even add. Yet Annie grasped the social function of literacy better than some "normal" students who had no idea why human beings would want to write at all. Annie understood that communication is more than a linguistic act and she was better than the average student at reading facial expressions, social cues, and the group affect. She had more empathy and less narcissism than many of her classmates. She was a mood barometer. Although she could not read, she loved being read to, and many classmates enjoyed reading to her, improving their own reading skills in the process. If English classes are about skill drills and knowing who Captain Ahab was, Annie doesn't belong. But if they are about understanding the full range of human communication and the role of stories in building relationships and communities, Annie belongs.

Annie had other characteristics that made her welcome in the classroom. She was relentlessly cheerful. She was always ready and willing to help anyone with anything. She always gave 100%. She always wanted to learn and please. What teacher doesn't dream of such students? She was also an outstanding artist. Having never lost the perspective and technique of a 4-year-old, she produced stunning children's art. Her primitive, snowman-like figures, colored with garish pinks, yellows, and blues, adorned many classroom walls. For her senior project, she painted a 10-foot by 12-foot mural on the wall outside my office.

None of us could imagine at the start of a course what Annie would contribute or produce. But she always contributed something and often produced charming booklets, poster board displays, or essays, dictated to other students. Like most students, she collaborated frequently. Unlike many students, she always had an impact on her collaborators. This is the most positive aspect of full inclusion: that by assuming ability to contribute, rather than inability, and assuming competence of some kind, rather than incompetence, you discover things about the disabled and nondisabled that you would never have discovered otherwise. We did not know what to expect of Annie, but we believed it was better to err on the side of possibility than of impossibility.

We were rewarded for that belief very quickly. Annie responded to the environment with an unprecedented explosion of verbal facility, memory gain, confidence, and personality. After 3 months, her agonizingly repetitive beginnings of sentences began to drop away. In school and at home, she spoke volumes more than before, spoke more appropriately, and spoke in longer sentences. She was far less passive, far more interactive. She began to ask questions—a far cry from parroting what others were saying. Six months later, she had exploded yet again.

I wish I could say that Annie's blossoming was the result of some particular programmatic strategy, beautifully carried out by a knowledgeable staff, but I can't. The truth is, we often did not know what to do with her, academically. We often thought we knew what to do, but did not have the time or resources to do it. We often felt that whatever we were doing, it wasn't enough or it wasn't right. We were often frazzled. We were starting a school from scratch, after all, and all of us had plenty to do besides think about Annie. This inability to treat her very differently from anyone else engendered some guilt, but, in hindsight, it might have been a blessing. The fact was, *none of us* were going to get all our needs met in those early months. Why should she be any different? And all of us were going to have to pitch in to do whatever needed to be done at the moment, or our community was not going to survive. Just like the rest of us, Annie had to vacuum, and take out the garbage, and paint, and entertain visitors, and schlep things around the school. Just like all the other students, Annie had to go on hikes and field trips and camping trips, whether she wanted to or not, whether it might be considered appropriate for her or not. We could not afford to lose or leave behind one person. We could not afford any specialists or prima donnas. It was truly all for one and one for all. Annie probably flowered as she did because we could *not* treat her as special.

P.S. 1 had no special educator for 2 years. We had parents who volunteered their expertise, including one, Mary Abbott, who was a special educator at another school. Our approach to Special Education was decidedly informal because the parents of SPED students at P.S. 1 wanted their children to be no more or no less special than any other children. I took my cues from them. Early on, when teachers could not think of something special for Annie to do, they let her trace letters in a first-grade penmanship book that a parent had provided. Although this activity might improve her eye–hand coordination, we all knew it was a pointless exercise.

Not only could she not remember how to do the letters once she left the letter book, she didn't know what to do with letters, even if she could create them. For a while, Mike and Marilyn hired a college student to come to school a few hours a week and read to Annie, play games with her, accompany her to class, and try to instill some number and letter sense in her. Sometimes either Marilyn or Mike would come in and work with Annie on her projects. Fellow students were always willing to work with her. She never seemed to mind when she was left to her own devices, as long as she was around other people.

When we had our first formal Special Education meeting about Annie—her annual review—we focused on four goals: building a circle of friends around Annie, getting her an internship at a child-care facility, experimenting with tape-recorded stories, and experimenting with whatever visual learning tricks we could think up. Her official IEP, from her last school, included a number of academic goals and objectives suitable for a first or second grader, but they were silly and had proven fruitless for years, so we ignored them. We reasoned that Annie was a teenager and should be treated like a teenager. Someone at the meeting said that our strategy should be to "fumble forward," and this football expression was as close as anything to the truth about what we were doing.

Both Mike and Marilyn were comfortable with fumbling forward and trusting the spirit of community to help Annie as much as any instructional program or assistive device (a tape recorder, for instance) we might employ. But Marilyn, it turned out, continued to hope against hope that Annie might somehow, some way, learn to read. Mike and I blabbed on and on about a general strategy of "growing dendrites"—stimulating Annie's brain in so many ways that her dendrites would multiply and intersect, with unpredictable positive results. But Marilyn continued to search for a breakthrough reading program or a reading guru who could somehow get Annie over the hump. One day, in Annie's third year, Marilyn came to me and spoke about this with more urgency and agitation than ever before. We could not go on with such general goals and so little structure to support Annie's learning to read, she said. We needed to focus more resources on Annie, the teachers needed to develop more formal curricular accommodations for Annie, we needed tutors for Annie who could *teach her to read*. I said that what she was describing was something we were not set up to accomplish at P.S. 1 and the thrust of it ran counter to what we had been doing for 3 years. I said that if she wanted all of those things, she probably should look for another school, because we just couldn't do them. She left unsatisfied, but never brought it up again. Years later, she told me that I had broken her heart that day. What she heard me say was, "Annie doesn't belong here."

I thought what I was saying was that the kind of intervention program Marilyn was describing didn't belong at P.S. 1. It never crossed my mind that Annie might not belong at P.S. 1. It was so obvious that she did. Annie became a fixture at P.S. 1, a leader in her peculiar way. This girl who walked funny, talked funny, and looked funny was teased only once that I can recall, and that was in the second month of school. The teaser was immediately put in his place by other students, and for the next 5 years, as the school quadrupled in size and all kinds of new students arrived, no one ever teased her again. New students could just tell it wasn't done and, if you did it, you would face some pretty tough kids. Annie was in school plays, school variety shows, dances, projects of all kinds, and community meetings. She had internships with little kids and the aged. She had sleepovers and parties at her house, and the parties were attended by popular and influential students. In her fourth year, she traveled with a group of students to the Canyonlands, leaving Mike and Marilyn behind. Mike was so worried about her that he arranged to drive over to Utah and meet the group, just to be sure she would be all right. When he showed up at the campfire, expecting her to be homesick and happy to see him, she said, "What are *you* doing here?" Mike spent the night and then drove back to Denver the next morning, both hurt and thrilled that she did not need him as much as he thought she did.

Annie clearly "belonged" at P.S. 1 and responded to the school's community spirit. But Annie was joined by Ben, who had a traumatic brain injury, and Sara, who had Down syndrome and Chris, who was autistic, and Nick, who had ADHD, and Martin, a manic depressive with an IQ of 160 and a history of debilitating migraine headaches, and dozens more students with dozens more ways of being different. Could full inclusion in a community meet their needs as well as it met Annie's? Would all parents of SPED students be as understanding and accommodating as this founding generation of parents, or would some begin to sue us? Could a system that depended so heavily on establishing close relationships survive rapid growth and change? Could teachers teach history or science or mathematics in a class that included not just Annie, but Sara and Ben and Chris and Nick and Martin and a half-dozen other "Spedheads" as well? Would well-disciplined, high-achieving students put up with rising proportions of disruptive and distracting students in their classrooms? Those were, and remain, the questions.

As P.S. 1 grew, so did its proportion of SPED students. In the third year, we hired a full-time special educator and two aides, one for Ben and one for Chris. The next year, we hired another full-time special educator. The school district took more of an interest in what we were doing and required more formal paperwork than we were used to doing, and this absorbed much of the special educators' time. Experienced teachers who believed completely in full inclusion began to complain about the difficulties of meeting the needs of such a range of students. Inexperienced teachers threw up their hands and questioned whether full inclusion could work even theoretically. It was certainly not something they were prepared to tackle. We had many success stories and many pleased parents, but we lost many students, too, because we could not find remedies for their problems fast enough. Everyone who visited the school remarked on its culture of diversity, inclusion, and caring, but some parents pulled their children out for fear they were being underchallenged in classrooms with too many inattentive, unruly, or disorganized peers. When the school's charter came up for renewal after 5 years, the school district insisted on taking over the Special Education programs in all its charter schools, lest a lawsuit bankrupt any of them or put the district in an untenable legal position. In addition, the district charged the school over $90,000 for its share of the district's "unfunded liability"—that is, the millions of dollars the district spends on SPED for which it is not reimbursed by either the state or federal government that mandated it.

7

Annie Green graduated on May 31, 2000. P.S. 1's sloppy, live-and-learn, community-oriented approach to full inclusion worked for her, and she now resides and works at the Camphill Soltane Community in Glenmoore, Pennsylvania. She has succeeded in life not because of experts or programs or legislation or litigation, but because of her own gifts and the support of caring people, exercising common sense.

As PL 94-142 approaches its thirtieth birthday, advocates for SPED have much to be proud of. Millions of children with learning problems have been singled out for attention and programming they otherwise might not have encountered. A profession largely oriented toward a mass production model of education has had to focus more of its energies on individualized learning. A system largely immune to scientific research has had to find ways to apply new findings about the human brain and how it works. Assistive learning technologies developed to help the few may well lead to breakthroughs for the many, just as curb cuts for the wheelchair-bound have been a boon to bicyclists and mothers with baby strollers. Children who might never have interacted with a disabled person have come to know and befriend many of them. A group of citizens once believed to be without their proper rights are now accorded them. A society whose ultimate strength depends on how it treats its weakest members can be said to be stronger.

We do not know the financial, social, and educational costs of this reform, but they appear to be staggering. The law, its consequent litigation, and its bureaucratic implementation have spawned massive inefficiencies and inequities. We do not know whom it has helped, whom it has hindered, and whether it has been effective. How do you evaluate the according of rights? How *can* you evaluate a highly individualized program that shrouds results in legal confidentiality, exempts students from regular testing, and focuses almost entirely on compliance with processes, not outcomes? What is the calculus necessary to sum up and weigh the joys of useful diagnoses against the damage done when children internalize the concepts of disability or victimhood? How many teachers have burned out in the effort to teach too great a range of learners? How many parents have pulled their children out of public schools because the classrooms contain too many disruptive students with real or imagined behavioral disorders?

Is it even fair of me to bring up the question of cost? I did not question the costs and benefits of school desegregation and integration. I had a school that was, and remains, beautifully diverse in all ways. I believe that diversity is a necessary precondition to a solid education as well as a requirement of a strong democracy. Yet I cannot put the rights of the "disabled"—a questionable label—on a par with the rights of disenfranchised ethnic minorities. To be sure, those rights have spawned their own programmatic burdens on schools, but few teachers question the presence of minorities in their classrooms or the importance of having a system that is wide open to all. That battle has been won. However, many teachers question their capacity to deal with the ever-increasing range of cognitive and emotional accommodations they must make in their classrooms and wonder whether the system as we know it can adapt to these demands without radical change. IDEA is about something more than rights. It is about the capacity of our education system to absorb and solve more and more of the social problems that broader communities are unable or unwilling to solve. How much more can we heap on our schools?

What can or should be done with SPED, as we know it? A number of scholars and policy makers are exploring options. G. Reid Lyon and his colleagues (2001) suggest major changes in how we define, diagnose, and remediate "learning disabilities." They point out that if schools and social agencies could put more effort into early prevention programs, fewer students would present themselves for SPED intervention later in life, when remediation becomes more expensive and less effective. They call for a cessation of current SPED identification practices that are clearly inadequate or based on specious inferences, such as the practice of assuming that if students are two grade levels behind their peers, or have a discrepancy between their IQ scores and their achievement, they must have a disorder of some kind. They argue that a new focus on preventing early reading problems could reduce the number of 12–17-year-olds identified as LD by 70%. They call for more precise, empirical definitions of learning disorders involving listening, speaking, arithmetic calculation, mathematics reasoning, and writing. All of these steps could be accelerated by changes in federal definitions, guidelines, and sanctioned programs.

We need to press for changes in SPED remediation practices, especially in reading, since typical SPED reading instruction is not markedly different from regular classroom practice and does not yield strong results (Klingner, Vaughn, Schumm, Hughes, & Elbaum, 1997; Torgesen et al., 2001). The long-term fix for ineffective SPED instruction is the same as the long-term fix for regular ineffective instruction: systemic changes that include new uses of student and teacher time, far more individualization of curriculum and instruction, continuous, on-site professional development, better use of instructional technology, a major overhaul of teacher education practices, and more small, community-oriented schools like P.S. 1.

If I could wave a magic wand and eliminate history, I would not tie this country's curriculum and instruction to the equal protections and due process clauses of the Fourteenth Amendment and would not base educational programs in civil rights legislation. The claim that individualized learning is a right available to some citizens but not others has more pernicious side effects than beneficial consequences for the community. Rights are absolute; learning is contingent on the interactions of flawed human beings, flawed institutions, and a host of unknown, and unknowable, variables. Education cannot rest on a legalistic foundation alone; it must be animated by a widely shared civic philosophy that tells us that we are all dependent on others when we are young, when we are old, when we are sick, and when we lack skills that others possess; and that every individual *must* contribute to his or her community if we are to be a great nation. Actions that grow out of such a philosophy are different from actions that grow out of legal wrangling. Curriculum, instruction, and placement decisions that grow out of such a philosophy are substantively different from curriculum, instruction, and placement decisions that emanate from legal mandates.

We face the risk that we will treat each other unfairly, regardless of whether we anchor our behavior in fear-based, compulsory

motives or motives rooted in mutual understanding of our interdependency. This is hard to judge, since unfairness means very different things in each system of thought. But at least it can be said
that a civic philosophy that highlights our interdependency entails
automatic solutions to apparent unfairness, whereas a legal decision only deposits the plaintiffs once again on the threshold of a
community that may or may not find a solution, depending on its
civic philosophy. Whatever we want to accomplish as a society—
legislatively or judicially—we have to accomplish it through communities. Everything depends on their health.

If our approach to learning problems were not based on rights,
the enormous weight currently placed on formal legal compliance
would lift, as would the enormous costs of a compliance-oriented,
high-litigation system. Billions and billions of dollars currently
tied up in paperwork and litigation might be spent, instead, on
helping all children learn. If our approach to apparent learning
problems were rooted in the understanding that we *all* have them,
to varying degrees and at varying times in our lives, curriculum
and instruction would change radically. The age-old dream of individualized education might one day be realized. Here, certainly,
SPED could be said to have paved the way. Indeed, that is the
direction in which I would send it and all its dollars. The barriers
to individualized education are political and cultural, not technical. The lock-step, general curriculum—which bores the prepared
student and "fails" the unprepared; which "covers" Asia today
and Africa tomorrow; which moves along in its peculiar sequence
and at its own pace, regardless of student interest or performance;
which is a mile wide and an inch deep; and which purports to be
essential for the creation of good workers and citizens—is a cultural artifact. No one seriously believes that all kids need to learn
the same things at the same time, day after day, or their lives will
be over before they start. What little research about learning there
is that can be used to support a lock-step curriculum can be used
as well to support many other approaches to education.

If Special Education became the research and development
arm of the education system, focusing not on learning "disorders,"
but on *learning in general*, and how to help *any* learner at any age

learn whatever he or she wants or needs to learn, in and out of school (why not in the workplace, too, or in underdeveloped countries?), it could accomplish its original goals and other social and economic goals besides. The rights question would necessarily shift, too. Now, a student must prove that he has a "disorder" relative to the lock-step curriculum and its demands, and special educators must find a solution relative to the lock-step curriculum and the traditional classroom (the "least restrictive environment"), wherein it is purveyed. It's all about getting them into that classroom where all the uniform, "normal," action is. What happens if that classroom is not normal in the sense that everyone there is getting something uniform, the denial of which to the SPED student would be detrimental to his education? What if all that was happening in the classroom was that students were learning different things at different paces and in different ways? And what if the "classroom" increasingly becomes any learning setting, anywhere? The essential "right" is not the right to be in a cookie-cutter classroom where everyone is plodding along the worn path of a dismal curriculum, but the necessity to *learn* in whatever way is best for an individual at a particular time. To the extent that education becomes increasingly individualized and settings for learning become increasingly diverse, the game changes for all students and the formulaic, rights-based approach to Special Education becomes less and less relevant.

If diagnosis were not focused on identifying more and more disorders, but instead were focused on determining how each student learns, then a SPED referral would be neither unusual nor stigmatizing. If it emerged that human beings had three or ten or fifteen major ways of learning, curriculum and instruction could be reconceptualized around those ways, plus independent study options, and no one would be a SPED student. When you redefine the curriculum, you redefine what it means to be out of sync with it. If everyone is learning something, and that is the point, then no one is out of sync, no one is "special."

I can still imagine special services for physically and mentally handicapped children. However, something has to be done about the mushrooming identification of "mild-to-moderate learning disabilities" and of emotional and behavioral "disorders." Department of Education figures show that since 1977, the proportion of students identified as having mild-to-moderate learning disabilities has grown 233%, while all other categories combined increased only 13%. No doubt much of this growth is due to the march of medicine. For example, medical success in saving low-birth-weight babies—who tend to have cognitive and neurological problems—ensures the presence of more students in schools who legitimately qualify for special services. Better and earlier medical diagnosis of neurological problems, deinstitutionalization of children with mental problems, and economic stress on families also contribute to rising numbers of legitimate candidates. Nevertheless, given the vagueness of this category, over 80% of all schoolchildren in the United States conceivably could qualify as having some kind of learning disability, simply because they are not "living up to their potential." The addition of ADD and ADHD diagnoses to this category, in 1999, and the fact that the funding formula provides strong incentives for schools to declare more and more underachieving students eligible, further expands the potential candidate pool beyond the bounds of common sense and affordability.

The question for a large number of these students is whether they are dysfunctional neurologically or their schools are dysfunctional academically and culturally. Large numbers of these students neither respect nor mind adults, do not comprehend and will not follow rules, and cannot interact productively with other children. Large numbers of schools neither respect nor listen to these kids, impose counterproductive "zero tolerance" rules on them, and cannot interact productively with their families. They condemn the students to medicalized discrimination, intellectually boring regimens, or continuous disciplinary action that ultimately leads to dropping out or expulsion.

This clash is less a medical problem than a class warfare problem. Schools are middle-class institutions that reached their present form without having to accommodate this kind of almost feral poor child and without having to tolerate "misbehavior" on this scale. School cultures must change as surely as curriculum and instruction must change. By school culture, I mean the entire system of incentives, expectations, relationships, conversations, and activities that make up the "informal" curriculum of the schools and establish the context for everyone's engagement in learning. We also have to face the fact that although every community can learn to deal with some of these students, no community can absorb large numbers of them and remain healthy. Schools with a critical mass of unsocialized, multiproblem students are categorically different from other schools and should be treated as such or closed, regardless of the political fallout.

SPED could be redesigned along lines sketched out above. It conceivably could become a gigantic national action-research project focused on how human beings learn. It conceivably could stimulate unprecedented experimentation in curriculum, instruction, and school culture. It conceivably could drive innovation and school reform for the next 25 years. It conceivably could make our schools more like healthy communities and our communities more like healthy schools. It conceivably could sow the seeds of a civic philosophy rooted in interdependency. The next trillion dollars we spend on Special Education conceivably could be the best trillion dollars this nation will ever spend. All this is conceivable, although not likely, without a massive commitment to a major reform of the whole system.

Annie Green's progress in life was conceivable, although not likely. It is best, I think, to take the same approach toward Special Education as we took toward Annie at P.S. 1: to err on the side of possibility. And when we ask ourselves how in the world we could move Special Education in the right direction, we should think of Annie's mantra: "It's right here . . . right here . . . right here: front of your face!"

CHAPTER 2

Full Moon Over Middle School

FULL MOON ACTIVITIES DAY!

Dear Students,

As today is a full moon day, we will suspend normal operations and instead follow the customary Full Moon Activities Schedule below. Have a good day!

7:30 a.m.: Outside Activities

Chasing, running, tripping, splitting lip on tetherball pole, skipping, jumping, slipping, bonging head on tetherball pole, colliding, scraping knees, scraping elbows, scrapping, tussling, grappling, wrestling, playing tag, tagging, sagging, running while sagging, falling down while running and sagging (because of the sagging), tearing, separating, straining, spraining, popping, breaking teeth on the tetherball pole, grinding asphalt into open wounds, skateboarding into traffic.

7:45 a.m.: Doors to school open

Chasing, running, tripping, splitting lip on drinking fountain, skipping, jumping, slipping, cracking head on desk, colliding, scraping knees, scraping elbows, scrapping, tussling, grappling, wrestling, playing tag, tagging, sagging, running while sagging, falling down while running and sagging (because of the sagging), tearing, separating, straining, spraining, popping, breaking teeth on the drinking fountain, grinding carpet into open carpet burns.

8:00 a.m.: Locker Activities

Banging, clanging, slamming, pounding, catching finger in locker being slammed by former friend, chasing former friend while screaming, screaming to be heard above the banging, clanging, slamming, and screaming, losing lock, forgetting combination of lock, putting lock on wrong locker, getting someone to cut your lock off with giant lock cutting tool, finding out that it wasn't really your lock that just got cut off, being threatened with giant lock cutting tool by angry owner of lock, losing key, cramming backpack into locker, cramming skateboard into locker, cramming books into locker, cramming case of Pepsi into locker, cramming little students into lockers.

8:15 a.m.: First Block: English, Social Studies, and History

Forgetting books, forgetting pencils, forgetting pens, forgetting homework, forgetting books AND pencils AND pens AND homework, forgetting what room the class is in, forgetting what seat is yours, forgetting what you learned yesterday, forgetting everything you've learned in your life, forgetting to turn off your pager, forgetting to turn off your walkman and leave it in your locker, remembering you were supposed to call your mother a half-hour ago, remembering where you left your bus pass and if you don't go there immediately it will be gone and you don't have any money and your mom will be mad at the school, remembering something you forgot and slapping your forehead, remembering you have to pee bad, discovering your braces are loose, discovering you have a pimple on the back of your neck, discovering girls, discovering boys, discovering you're getting your period, discovering your homey is having her period and you have to go with her to the girls room, pestering, gesturing, poking, pinching, making honking noises, drooling on purpose, smearing antibiotic cream on your festering navel-piercing wound, saying, "I don't know" whenever asked a question, saying, "I know! I know!" with your hand way up and jumping up and down in your seat and then forgetting the answer when called upon, saying, "Why do you always call on me?" saying, "This is boring," saying, "This is

pointless," saying, "This is stupid," saying, "This is boring, pointless, and stupid."

9:45 a.m.: Break

Munching Cheetos, crunching Doritos, punching kid with
mouth full of Cheetos, hunching in corner with snack from mom;
swilling, chilling, drilling kid with mouthful of peanuts, spilling
Pepsi, spilling Coke, spilling orange drink, spilling Dr. Pepper,
spilling guts, scoffing down, scarfing, devouring, masticating
(mouth closed), masticating (mouth wide open), chewing quietly,
chewing loudly; chugging, glugging, guzzling, swigging, sucking,
nibbling, gnawing, choking, cramming, gagging, spitting, spew-
ing, hurling, puking in the drinking fountain.

10:00 a.m.: Second Block: Science and Mathematics

Writing your name all over your books with a leaky ball point,
writing your homey's name all over your books, writing your
squeeze's name on the desk, writing notes on your palm, writing
on your forearm, writing on your tongue, writing on your jeans,
scribbling, doodling, defacing tables with compass points, deepening holes in desk that someone else started, using locker key;
drawing pistols with smoke coming out the barrel and a spinning
bullet headed toward someone's head, drawing huge machine
guns spraying bullets everywhere, drawing people with big holes
in their heads and plus signs for eyes, drawing grim, overmuscled
superheroes with spears, drawing angry, overbreasted super-
heroines with whips, drawing snarling dogs, drawing snarling
cats, drawing unidentifiable things eating other unidentifiable
things, drawing Japanese anime characters, drawing lumpy cars
with weapons all over them, drawing sleek cars, drawing cars
crashing and heads coming out the windshields, drawing severed
fingers, drawing fists, drawing hands making gang signs, drawing
tags, drawing indecipherable graffiti messages, drawing virgin
sacrifices, drawing big hearts with tears falling and little daggers
all around, drawing portraits of self with huge, innocent eyes,
drawing portraits of self as a devil.

Chewing gum, chewing paper, chewing Cheetos bags, chewing pencils, chewing pens, chewing rulers, chewing protractors, chewing erasers, chewing calculators, chewing fingernails, gnawing on the desk like a beaver, sucking ink out of ball point pen, sucking on cheeks, sucking on knuckles, sucking hard candy, sucking breath mints, sucking Pez; picking nose, picking ears, picking scabs, pricking arms and sucking blood, sniffing wrist, unconsciously twirling hair around and around index finger, stroking hair, smoothing hair, putting hair up, taking hair down, pulling hair in front of face and examining it closely, braiding homey's hair, brushing homey's hair, picking hair, adjusting bandana, adjusting black pantyhose cap that makes you look like a criminal, adjusting shower cap, adjusting sweatshirt hood so no one can see your eyes, retreating deep inside XXL Dallas Cowboys down jacket where no one can see you or hear you, staring at own midriff like it's someone else's.

11:30 a.m.: Sustained Silent Reading

Reserve seat on grimy, gritty couch for homey, punch kid who takes the seat anyway and cite Byzantine rules about couch seating, forget book, forget magazine, forget comic book, wander the school looking for new book, read skateboard catalogue, lay on couch reading, lay on kids who are sitting on couch reading, lightly tickle inner arm of couch mate while reading, lay on the floor reading, lay on the desk reading, huddle up underneath the stairs reading, slouch in chair reading, tip back in chair reading, read yourself to sleep, just read, little angels, just read.

12:00 noon: Lunch

Beg friends for lunch money, shake kids down for lunch money, spend lunch money on candy and pop, beg teachers for money, beg school secretary for money, overturn couch cushions looking for lunch money, promise to do anything for lunch money, loan lunch money at exorbitant rates, tell cafeteria lady that you're eligible for free lunch but your name is missing from the list because your mother changed her name, say you paid extra last week and it's not your fault the school lost the paperwork, say your mom's bringing money after school, tell the cafeteria lady you're somebody who happens to be absent today, make the cafeteria lady pity you, eat off other people's plates, eat food left on the table, eat food off the floor.

Suck, gurgle, gulp, burp, lick, lip, chew, gnash, guggle, mouth, bolt, salivate, sneeze on your cheese, wheeze on your cheese whiz; scoop your pudding with your fingers, wipe your fingers on a napkin, wipe your fingers on your shirt, wipe your fingers on someone else's shirt, wipe your fingers on the table, wipe your fingers underneath the table, don't wipe your fingers at all; slurp your pudding, slurp your soup, slurp your milk, slurp your chocolate milk, wipe your mouth with your shirt, wipe your mouth with someone else's shirt; crunch, munch, punch while munching, nudge a pudgy kid while he's sucking on his fudge; blow straw wrapper wads at neighbor's eyes, blow straw wrapper wads in neighbor's pudding, inhale straw wrapper wads, trade orange for candy bar, trade banana for candy bar, trade apple for candy bar, trade anything nutritious for anything made of sugar, play cheese-slice Frisbee, shoot at cheese-slice Frisbee with straw wrapper wad, wipe mayo off bread slice using edge of table, double fold peanut butter sandwich and eat it with one bite, roll peanut butter sandwich into ball and eat it with one bite, turn peanut butter sandwich inside out and eat it without hands; splash, drip, spill, tip, stain, break, burst, slop, mess, crumb up, stick, slick up, hiccup, pour on the floor, slide on banana, glide on pudding, dip chips, drip dip, slip on the dip.

12:40 p.m.: Third Block: Electives

Ditch, come late because you had to visit your aunt at the hospital, come late because you were with your father only he forgot to give you a note, come late because your homey has her period, come late because lunch made you sick, come late because you had a straw wrapper wad in your eye, come late because lunch period is too short and you were the last one served and it's the school's fault, come late reeking of tobacco, come late reeking of dope, come late reeking, sneak in, squeak in, peek in, ditch.

Sleep with eyes open, sleep with eyes alternately closing slowly and then popping open wildly, sleep with head nodding slowly forward then snapping back, sleep with head on forearm on desk, sleep face first on desk with arms hanging down to floor, sleep tipping back in chair with head against the wall, doze, snore, snort, dream, hallucinate.

2:00 p.m.: Last Block: Interdisciplinary Projects

Glue stuff, screw stuff, get blue stuff on your blouse; pound, saw, nail, staple, tape, drape, mount, rout, miter, clamp, tamp down, shore up, paint, draw, cut, paste, stencil, chalk, wire, fire up, model in clay, model in papier mache; look at microbes through microscope, look at microbes swimming in your spit, look at snot through microscope, extract earwax from reluctant donor and look at it through microscope; search internet for "buck nekkid," search Internet for "fart," search Internet for "boner," find bulimia chat line and pretend you have bulimia, repeat process for anorexia, lupus (even though you don't know what lupus is), impotence, and bad PMS; continue Internet chat with girl in Detroit who thinks you are a high school senior, hack into the school intranet, hack into the library database and eliminate your fines for overdue books, hack into the Pentagon and launch a missile. Leave early because you have to take the early bus because your grandmother is ill, leave early for an orthodontist appointment, leave early for private dance/piano/Akido lessons, leave early because you have to decorate for a dance, leave early because your homey has to decorate for a dance and you have to help her, leave early because you have to go to Mexico for a few weeks.

3:45 p.m.: Dismissal

See 7:30 a.m. for appropriate behavior.

TEACHER SCHEDULE

6:00 a.m.: Awake in cold sweat, get out of bed, never having slept; throw up, calm jitters with pot of coffee, take extra Prozac, take extra Valium, look in mirror and chant, "I can do this!" 50 times, call in sick, call in tired, call in sick and tired, take "mental health" day, gear up, psych up, gird loins, prepare for the worst, man the torpedoes, lock and load.

7:30 a.m.–3:45 p.m.: Persevere, hold out, hang on, hang tough, hang five, hang out, let it all hang out, hang 'em high, hang in there; outwit them, out think them, outlast them, rout the pouters; stay the course, steady as she goes, all hands on deck, luff the mizzens, avast! Avast! Every man for himself, row, man, row for your life! Dive! Dive! Incoming! Incoming! Medic! Medic! *I can't take it anymore! I can't take it anymore!*" (slap, slap), "Pull yourself together, man, you've got a job to do!" Count on each other, count on me, count the days until your paltry retirement, mount up, rally, circle those wagons, praise God and pass the ammunition, you're going to make it, you're one minute closer, there's light at the end of the tunnel, teach on, teach on, with hope in your heart and you'll never teach alone, at the end of the day there's a golden something or other and the sweet tender song of a lark—do you hear it? Do you hear the lark? It's singing to you over the slamming of the lockers, the shouts and screams and shrieks, its song grows louder, it's climbing into the rafters, it's soaring above the smoking battlefield, it's the most beautiful sound in the world, *it's the dismissal bell!* Oh my god! Oh my God! We've done it! We've come through!

FACULTY MEETING: AGENDA

1. Old business, very old business, extremely very old business, Babylonian business, Paleolithic business, business dating from the Big Bang.
2. Unresolved issues, unanswered questions, untenable ideas, unlikely hopes (unappetizing food, uncomfortable little chairs, unfriendly looks), unfortunate assertions, unconsciousness, unintelligible gibberish.
3. Reports.
    a. *Discipline Committee*
       Display of contraband from locker sweep: headphones, spray paint, bong, sizable block of hash.

Whining, self-pity, fear, shock, "concern," horror, teeth gnashing (noshing, noshing while gnashing), hand wringing, total amnesia, self-righteousness, we don't get no respect, where are the "consequences"? Motion to purchase stun guns, fist fight between proponents of structure and proponents of permissivism, blaming the parents, blaming the kids, blaming the principal.

b. *Curriculum Committee*

Whining, self-pity, shocking ignorance, blaming the parents, blaming capitalism, blaming the principal. Lighting the bong "to see what it's like."

c. *Testing Committee*

Whining, self-pity, anxiety, regression, paranoia, blaming the district, blaming the legislature, blaming the principal. Coughs, giggles, grins, guffaws. More noshing. Motion to accelerate passing of the bong. Cheers, toasts, birdsong imitations.

d. *Instructional Improvement Task Force*

Whining, self-pity, lecturing, hectoring, oratory, rude noises, humming, peace signs, motion to praise the Oreos, bad posture, chirping.

e. *Sexism and Harassment Task Force*

Whining, self-pity, catcalls, quacking, honking, barking, mooing.

4. New Business

Motion to make a motion to make a motion to make a motion, discussion of motion to make a motion to make a motion to make a motion, point of clarification about motion, discussion of clarification, clarification of discussion of clarification, move the question, question the move, clarify the question, move the moving of the question, braying, crowing, clucking, snorting, screeching, shouting, "I've got the answer!" shouting, "Wait! Wait! I've got the answer," shouting, "Everybody! Listen! I've got the answer" until everyone is suddenly quiet and then shouting, "What? What?"

Adjourn.

PHONE MESSAGES

7:00 a.m.: "Garblegarble screech won't be in today. He has pink eye."

7:01 a.m.: "Screechscreechmumble car won't start so she'll be late."

7:03 a.m.: "Gorgleburgle forgot his lunch. Mzzims will drop by to give the lunch money to vvvvvmeyer."

7:09 a.m.: "Dr. Brown? Mary gjkan. Laura never came home last night. Will you call me if she shows up at school? 297-jch8bor9. Thank you."

7:14 a.m.: " . . . huh? . . . (dialtone)."

7:21 a.m.: "Is there a human being at this school? Do I always have to talk to a machine? Is anybody there? Do you know your answering machine still wishes people a happy holiday? DON'T YOU KNOW WHAT TIME OF YEAR IT IS? DO YOU KNOW HOW IRRITAT-ING screechclick."

7:22 a.m.: "I'M TRYING TO LEAVE A MESSAGE FOR SOMEONE, ANYONE TO TELL MY SON TO GO TO HIS MOTHER'S INSTEAD OF screechclick."

7:23 a.m.: "Mr. Brown, this is Alice in the Superintendent's office. Dr. Eckerling MUST see you at 10:00. It's very important. Please let me know that you can make it. Thank you."

7:23 a.m.: "Dr. Brown, this is Mary Gallegos. Hector came home yesterday with pink eye and it looks worse this morning, so please excuse him. Thank you."

7:24 a.m.: " . . . JUST NEED TO KNOW THAT YOU WILL TELL TOM THAT HE HAS TO GO TO HIS screechscreech GOD DAMN IT! . . . click."

7:40 a.m.: "This is Don ardlvshr. I just want to confirm our 10:00 meeting regarding your asbestos management plan. Thank you."

7:43 a.m.: "This is Molly Venor. Melissa's eyes are all puffy and there's crusty stuff in the corners and I'm going to take her to the doctor's this morning. Thank you."

7:45 a.m.: "This is Vernon Light's father. I got your call and I'll be in at 10:00 to meet with you. See you then."

8:00 a.m.: "Good morning. This is Christina Poppe at the Department of Education. We sent you forms for your teachers to fill out 6 weeks ago and they were due last week and we have not received them. Would you please screechclick."

8:05 a.m.: "Honey? The plumber called and said he could be here at 10:00. I'm going to be at Barbara's. I told him you'd run home and let him in. I know it's a bother, but it's the only time he could make it. Thanks. Loveyou."

8:10 a.m.: "Garblegarble Health Department. I'm calling in response to your letter about the milkolator. Please call me at 303 5shzoo4143."

8:22 a.m.: "Hi, Rex, it's John. I'm having coffee with Kay, the new board member, and I thought I'd bring her over to the school. Mid-morning, probably, about 10:00. See you then."

Ddzzzshzzshscreeeeeeeeeeeeeeeeeeeeeeeeeeeeeeeeeeeeeee (flashing red light) beepbeepbeepbeepbeepbeep . . .

NOTES LEFT ON CHAIR (IN REVERSE ORDER)

Someone took my keys. House keys, car keys. Also had the van keys and the school master key on the ring. Change the locks again?

Kirsten

Rex,

You need to know that I am setting limits. I can do just so much. WE HAVE TO TALK!

L

Rex,

The auditor wants to know (a) how we spent the leftover CDE money (b) where the receipts are for last summer's retreat (c) where's the documentation for the anonymous grant? ASAP

Cindy

Girls toilet backed up (stall 3).
WE HAVE TO TALK!

L

Need a sub for this afternoon. Pink eye.

Eric

Guy from lighting company stopped by. Says our kids were running around on his roof. Very angry.

Rainy

CALL SUPT.!

Rainy

Slight gas smell coming from furnace room. Call somebody?

Joe

CALL ASBESTOS GUY! Says he had an appt.

Rainy

CALL MR. LIGHT! Very angry.

Rainy

Caught off campus: Melissa, Tyler, Rage, and Desi.

Jen

Caught smoking: Peter, Jamiliah, Caira.

Paul

Stopped by with new board member. Sorry we missed you.

John

CALL HOME!

Rainy

Auditor needs info ASAP!

Cindy

DICTATION TAPE

" . . . uh, let's see . . . "

CHAPTER 3

Serving Time

1

"Live and learn," goes the adage. It is difficult for us to separate learning from living, so central is learning to the experience of being human. We are learning machines from birth until death. We are creatures who must learn or perish.

Much of that learning seems preprogrammed: learning to speak, for instance, or learning to walk. Much of it seems effortless and natural, hardly requiring any obvious tutoring or reflection. Think of all the things children learn in their first 5 years: family history, primitive science and mathematics, language, morality, complex social behaviors, how to play and tell stories, a stunning number of facts, concepts, skills, virtues, and mores—and they learn these things by themselves, around family members and in groups, informally.

In most cultures, adults give children ample time to reach various important cultural learning milestones, not worrying much about variations of months and even years in the progress of individuals. They are allowed long periods of time to learn to hunt or gather food or acquire the arts of storytelling. Parents expect that it takes many years for wisdom to grow, for spiritual insight to ripen, for learning the value of courage or humility or steadfastness. It seems that for many important accomplishments, there is a fullness of time to learn.

Modern school learning, in contrast, is rigorously paced, timed to the minute. In part, this reflects a social recognition that, at around age 5, childhood moves into a stage when young people need more disciplined kinds of play, finer tuning of skills, more responsibility. For older students, the increasing intrusion of time-pressure into learning is acculturation into the probability of an adult work life dominated by the clock. But schooling's pace is also a consequence of the way the enterprise is organized, not unlike an early-twentieth-century factory, with its production lines, managers' concerns about output, and accountants' conviction that "time is money."

Whatever the reasons, young people in the United States are required by law to be in school a certain number of hours per day, days per year, and total years. Students who enter in a particular year are expected to stay together and march along in tandem toward graduation 13 years later. In elementary schools, students must study mathematics and reading so many minutes a day; later, each course consumes a certain number of "credit hours" ultimately necessary for graduation. Courses thus are broken into units and lessons, subjects are sequenced, to consume certain proportions of the available time. Days are broken into 44-minute periods, and periods are further subdivided. Bells ring all day to demarcate various transitions. Tests are timed, students first to get their hands up are called upon, speed is everywhere seen as a virtue. It is not enough to know the answer; you must know it sooner than someone else. To be called "slow" is to have one's intelligence called into question. If a student has not learned a certain skill by a certain time, he is suddenly "behind." With luck, he might get into an "accelerated" class and catch up. Many parents are worried when their child is reading at grade 4, month 6, but his friends are reading at grade 4, month 9, or even grade 5 or higher. It is a catastrophe, even for the most progressive parents, to have a child who is not reading at all by grade 3.

Driving the whole time-based education system is the widely shared belief, reinforced by law and custom, that the bulk of an American's education must be accomplished between the ages of 5 and 18. At that point, all Americans are expected to enter the workforce, the military, or some form of postsecondary education leading to a credential worth more on the labor market than a mere high school degree. Although it is acceptable to enter postsecondary schools at any point in one's life and to stay as long as one can afford it, it is not acceptable to stay in high school indefinitely or return after the age of 18 or 19.

This cap on the duration of preparatory schooling forces educators automatically to break any subject into 12 year-long units of study, break the years into 180 days, break the days into minutes, and then plot out a sequence of teaching activities that seem to make sense within that framework. If society gave them 20 years, they would break a subject into twenty units; if given 6 years, they would break a subject into six yearly units. These divisions have nothing to do with the structure of knowledge. Nor are they based on what we know about the nature of learning. They are arbitrary accommodations to the given amount of time allowed for attaining a license to work or enter the military or go on to college. If we designed a system of *learning*, instead of a system of schooling, time might be used in a different, and ultimately more effective, way.

Is our current approach to formal learning one we would use if we had the opportunity to redesign it? Is there some other approach that might be less rigidly time-bound, and at least as efficient? How much time do people really need to learn important skills, concepts, and habits of mind? How might learning time be changed or reconceived in order to better educate a wider range of citizens? Should our schools offer more time or less time or a different kind of time for learning? Is there a way to get more learning packed into shorter or equal amounts of time?

The fate of the current movement to reform and restructure the public schools depends on answers to these kinds of questions, for to reform the current system is ultimately to redefine and reshape the existing relationships between time and learning.

2

Since schooling is organized so tightly around time, one would think educators know a great deal about the relationships between time and learning. After all, how could educators sequence learning for children, determine how many lessons to give each week, create textbooks, give lectures, set up laboratories, and so forth, and not know, at least on average, how much time it takes to learn each fact, concept, or skill?

But in fact, we have very little empirical knowledge about such things. Educators haven't the faintest idea how long it "should" take to learn how to draw or learn the Pythagorean theorem or understand the issues behind the Civil War. It depends on what one means by learning and on how one might propose to control the many variables that individuals bring to learning experiences that account for the time it takes for each to learn any particular concept or skill to any particular degree of depth.

Informal learning is not very problematic: Young people are learning all the time, because that's what young human beings do. But as soon as learning becomes formal, problems arise. Teachers need to define learning very precisely and relate it to what they happen to be teaching. But it is difficult to say where learning starts or stops, whether it will take place now or later, whether it is shallow or deep. It is as if each child were a meandering river: Adults stand beside the river drawing lines in the water where they want one kind of learning to end and another to begin, throwing objects in, observing whether they float down the river on one current or up on an eddy. The river goes where it must go, as teachers try to dam it here, deepen it there, send it where they want it to go. Their professional esteem rests on the belief that they can make students learn what they want them to learn at any given moment. They must find evidence that students learned what they taught them, regardless of the difficulties.

In such circumstances, it seems sensible to define learning as an activity that leads to knowing. If someone knows something, then it may be fair to infer that he or she must have learned it. If I have *taught* something and I want to determine whether you have *learned* it, I could assess your *knowledge* of the subject. Knowing, we could tell ourselves, is learning made visible; knowing is having learned.

But knowing and learning are clearly different states. I can say, "I am learning to ride a bicycle," not, "I am knowing to ride a bicycle." Learning suggests incompleteness, a continuing quest and images of people trying, fumbling, wondering, not getting it, furrowing their brows. Knowing suggests arrival, possession, an achieved state, and images of people operating on their knowledge, performing routines, acting on what they know. Knowledge does not necessarily derive from a formal learning process. Some knowledge, for instance, is built into the brain; some emerges spontaneously from conversations and situations; much of it is tacit and unspecifiable; much of it happens in our minds as a sudden synthesis of countless, unrelated bits of information, long after overt attempts to "teach" those bits to us.

Learning is clearly about much more than acquiring knowledge. Often, the formal knowledge gained from casting about, making theories, interpreting events, and trying to solve problems is of minor importance. Often, our efforts to describe the knowledge supposedly gained from a learning experience are failures; we don't really *know* what we learned. Often, when we retrospectively reconstruct how we have come to know something, we make up a story. We don't really know how we came to know something. Reducing learning to "knowledge acquisition" is like reducing loving to mate acquisition. There's a relationship, all right, but something critical gets lost in the reduction.

Learning, when it is confused with knowledge acquisition, loses its active, open-ended qualities and becomes mere repetition. Teaching becomes a circle that begins with the teacher's given knowledge and ends with the repetition of that same knowledge by the student. Learning gets lost by being "assumed" to have taken place. It receives little direct attention. Acts of discovery, invention, and interpretation escape notice, while the routines of knowledge manipulation move to center stage. Since the full act of learning includes purposes for doing so and personal commitments to do so, a reduction of the act to a list of knowledges gained, or goals and objectives met, deprives the learner of the only things that might give that knowledge meaning.

We have a system in which knowledge is the object of our attention, and learning is the (largely invisible) handmaiden of knowledge. Perhaps that is why the knowledge students gain in school means so little to them and is so useless to them in any context but schooling. What if we said that knowing is just a stage in learning? That knowledge isn't the end point of anything, but always a starting point (as in "the more I know, the more I know I don't know")? This may sound like a chicken and egg situation, philosophically, but where you put your focus practically, makes a big difference: A chicken is *not* an egg. A system of education that puts knowing first and assumes learning, is not the same as a system that puts learning first and asks knowing to be the handmaiden. The systems not only would be substantively different, but would treat and allocate time differently.

We get closer to the crucial difference when we go beyond the concept of knowing to the concept of understanding. It's one thing to "know" that Einstein came up with the formula "E = mc squared," but quite another thing to understand what he really meant; one thing to know who Captain Ahab was, another thing to understand *Moby Dick*; one thing to know Lincoln's Gettysburg Address by heart, another to understand the Civil War. As David Perkins (1992) and others have pointed out, one who understands something is able to go beyond the information given, able to explain things about a concept, demonstrate it in various ways, argue about it, and *apply* it in different circumstances.

When we define learning as not simply knowing about something, but understanding it and being able to apply it in new situations; and when we throw the spotlight on the features, processes, and techniques of learning, of constantly expanding knowledge, we undermine the whole system of contemporary education. Time for worthwhile learning is different from time for mere knowledge acquisition. To put the spotlight on learning is also to illuminate the conditions necessary for learning: motivation, fluency in the language of instruction, foundational knowledge on which to build, context, certain inquiry and thinking processes, appropriate environments and opportunities, to name a few major contributors.

It follows from what we know about key factors that, ideally, for each lesson to be learned, a student needs time to be motivated; time to become fluent in the language of instruction; time to acquire foundational content and process knowledge; time to place new knowledge in personal and social contexts; time to theorize, practice, and be exposed to many different opportunities to learn the knowledge in question; time to develop a certain kind of trust; time to understand and time to apply; time to read about it, write about it, discuss it, model it, make mistakes, get lost and find the way out; time to compare new knowledge with primitive knowledge, schema, and theories; and time to discover, inquire further, argue, and solve problems in novel situations.

Obviously, these amounts of time are going to vary for each student. Real learning is idiosyncratic. No one can know how much time it will take any particular student to understand or apply any particular lesson. Any organization of lessons is necessarily arbitrary and capricious at worst, notional (e.g., "this is about how much time it *should* take," or "this is how much time it took last year") at best. In such circumstances, and given the pressure to deliver education within a circumscribed period, public education has taken what appears to be a perfectly sensible course. It has said, in effect, "This is how much time we're going to *give* you, and we hope it works out for most of you." It provides the timed curriculum, and students either adjust to it or do not.

In this respect, public mass education has been organized like public mass transportation. Unable to predict or serve door to door all the transportation needs of everyone in the city, mass transit planners set up a grid that enables them to serve most neighborhoods at intervals that seem reasonable to them, given the fiscal restraints of running a transit system and information about where and when people tend to want to go. "This is when our buses run and these are the places where you can catch them," the transit people say. "If you're in the right place at the right time, the bus will stop and pick you up. If you miss the bus, that's your lookout. Another will be along after a while. This is how we run our buses. It's up to you to catch them."

So it is with public mass education. We say, in effect, "Here are the lessons we teach, here are the amounts of time we allocate to each lesson, get on board. If you miss something, that's your lookout. It'll probably be repeated. This is how we teach. It's up to you to learn."

Such an approach is inherently fair from the point of view of the public interest, unfair from the point of view of individuals and certain groups. Some individuals and groups of people live closer to the bus stops, want to go where the buses go, and find the schedule matches their needs well. Other individuals and groups live farther from the bus stops, are not going where the buses go, and find the schedules inconvenient.

Some students arrive at school fluent in the language of instruction, accustomed to family conversations that are similar to classroom conversations, and filled with cultural background knowledge that is foundational for school learning. Such children do not require as much time to learn as students who do not know the language, have not had school-like family conversations, and do not possess the background knowledge their teachers assume they possess. Yet all are expected to move through lessons and through the system at pretty much the same pace, graduating with their cohorts. Profound stigmatism is attached to falling behind a grade and not graduating with one's peers.

In an effort to deal fairly with this, the school system has created different "tracks," "ability groups," "compensatory" courses, and "remedial" programs, all of which vary the content of lessons and the amount of time (within limits) afforded students to learn. It is widely observed that students who go into the slower learning channels seldom return to "regular-time" learning. This is no wonder. So long as regular-time learning (however arbitrarily conceived) continues in its lock-step progression (built into the required curriculum), students who are diverted to slower coursework seldom will be able to catch up. It is as if there were two moving sidewalks, one moving twice as fast as the other, and some students were taken off the fast sidewalk for a while to walk on the slow sidewalk; even if you eventually put them back on the fast sidewalk, their classmates would be far ahead of them and would stay there. Catching up requires far greater effort, far more time, than the students who usually are asked to catch up tend to have at their disposal.

So long as the required curriculum is a *timed* curriculum, to which the student must adjust (like a bus schedule), and so long as some students come to school requiring longer periods of time to acquire the background knowledges and skills the curriculum assumes they have—just so long will schooling continue to be an inequitable social sorting institution. The phrase "equal opportunity" means nothing if it does not mean equal opportunity to learn; and opportunity to learn means nothing if it does not mean that each child is entitled to the *time* it takes him or her to learn.

The timed curriculum is a response to the batch processing demands of mass education. Everyone knows that in any given class, some students will find the pace of instruction too fast, some, too slow. Schooling is about moving along at an average pace determined by what seems to have "worked" for a politically acceptable proportion of students over a number of years. To cover its bets, the system repeats an enormous amount of material. Various aspects of grammar, for instance, are taught virtually all 12 years; the mathematics curriculum incorporates great redundancy, repeating two-thirds of the previous year's curriculum in some years. Students who pick up the lessons the first time find much of their class time boring. Students who do not learn the material the first few times it is presented (always in the same way) begin to think they are not smart enough to learn it. When it becomes clear that they will not graduate with their peers, they drop out.

Anyone who observes classroom instruction in typical schools is struck by the amount of potential time for learning that is squandered on noninstructional activities. Most of this squandered time is another consequence of batch processing. Because a teacher is trying to move 30 students along at the same pace, she spends a great deal of time giving directions, controlling the restless, lecturing (not a very efficient way to transmit knowledge), and conversing with one student while 29 do little or nothing. Numerous interruptions (e.g., loudspeaker announcements, fire drills) consume more precious learning time.

Studies historically have shown large differences in how time is allocated from school to school. Some schools provide almost 60% more raw learning time than others (Kemmerer, 1978–1979; Smith, 2000). Only a fraction of that raw time is "engaged" time, or "time-on-task," which also varies widely from classroom to classroom, and school to school (Berliner, 1979; Rosenshine, 1980). And only a fraction of engaged time is truly productive time, that is, leads to long-term learning (Walberg, 1988).

Many teachers recognize the waste and try to individualize learning time as much as they can within the constraints imposed by the overall school schedule. They ask students to fill in worksheets independently while they move from student to student, offering different kinds of advice. They divide students into small activity groups and move from group to group. They assign work that students do at home and they correct at home. They ask students to keep learning journals and logs, to write independently and evaluate one another's writing. They organize cooperative learning groups within which students collaborate and teach each other.

These efforts to maximize learning time for individuals have been shown to improve achievement somewhat, but they only expand the learning time within particular lessons and units, which remain embedded in the larger curricular sequence and schedule. Tenth-grade, credit-hour requirements are still in place; the tenth-grade American literature survey still must begin with the Puritans and end with a contemporary writer, touching Emerson, Thoreau, Longfellow, Whitman, Melville, and numerous other writers along the way. Coverage of the curriculum remains the imperative. Learning activities that consume time (writing, discussion, inquiry, argument, projects)—activities that deepen understanding—take a backseat to activities that keep things moving along, regardless of how shallow the learning is. To inquire or discuss or elaborate too much is to risk not covering the "material" (largely facts) that ultimately will be tested through nationally standardized tests, state assessments, and college entrance examinations, all of which are designed on the assumption that the material *has* been covered.

3

Because learning is partly a function of interactions between young people and adults, how adult time is structured in schools and school districts strongly affects how much learning is likely to take place. The adults have created a certain kind of organization for their work, the major characteristics of which are a highly detailed structure of specialized jobs; clear, top-down lines of command; centralized organizational goals, objectives, and activities, established by constant rational planning; and numerous forms of credentialing, coordination, accountability, and control.

This combination of organizational structures—we'll call it the mechanistic/bureaucratic organization—has obvious strengths if the purpose of the organization is to manufacture a uniform product or deliver a standardized service in a stable economy or relatively static social environment. It works well in a labor market with a surplus of workers who will follow orders and perform minutely defined tasks repetitively, under the guidance of middle managers who are, themselves, carrying out predetermined ends. It makes sense for the military and, during the Industrial Age, it made sense for many businesses. For much of the twentieth century, many people believed that any large undertaking necessarily would be organized in this general way.

Clearly, such a form of organization could be run well or poorly, could use time and materials efficiently or wastefully. But even at its best, such an organization suffers from glaring weaknesses. When the tasks it is to perform become too numerous or complex, when the environment around it becomes unpredictable, when its customers change their expectations, and when the labor market no longer supplies sufficiently compliant workers, such an organization becomes increasingly inefficient in its use of time and resources. Not designed for innovation, it cannot keep up with the times. Not designed to meet new needs, it becomes increasingly isolated from its clients or customers. Broken into tiny subunits within which people cannot see the whole picture, the organization tends to ignore new problems or attack them in piecemeal ways that make things worse.

Our school system is based heavily on this model of organization, and it suffers mightily from its weaknesses. Although some school districts and schools manage their use of time better than others, the organizational structure itself is out of sync with the times and severely limited in its capacity to use worker time efficiently, let alone provide the kinds of time necessary to enable all students to learn. Consider the many ways in which time can be squandered in the mechanistic/bureaucratic organization.

- Because they have become their own self-sustaining bureaucracies, many school districts have become closed to the communities around them. In the process, educators not only have become incapable of responding to their clients' needs, but have become incapable of using the 87% of time that students spend outside of school for learning opportunities.

Moreover, the bunker mentality that prevails in many large central administrations costs both short-term and long-term time. In the short term, paranoia, defensiveness, and resistance translate into meetings, paperwork, and political squabbling that could be better spent on matters affecting learning. In the long term, the more an organization drifts out of sync with its purposes, the more complex, costly, and time-consuming will be its day of reckoning.

- Centralized planning, by which the few tell the many what to do, brings with it a compliance mentality, by which the few try to determine whether the many did what they were told to do. The combination can lead to enormous wastes of time in endless re-planning of plans that weren't very realistic, constant sabotage of plans by people who were not involved in the planning, proliferating regulation to ensure that people follow through on plans, elaborate grievance procedures for people who don't want to do what the planners planned, mountains of paperwork for everyone involved, and so much time going into the routines of compliance that there is no time for thinking about how to do things more efficiently.

Planning, of course, requires a grasp of the changes going on around the organization and accurate predictions about the future. Unfortunately, the bureaucratic school district is out of touch with its environment and cannot make accurate predictions. Managers spend time trying to force implementation of plans that are no longer relevant and creating new plans that also will not be relevant. The preferred method of rational planning, which begins always with the last plans and the perceptions of bureaucrats, not learners, allows no room for ideas or perspectives that might introduce creative solutions to chronic problems.

In organizations committed to rational planning and management, high value is placed on predictability, objectivity, logic, and certainty. Ironically, learning is unpredictable, highly subjective, not entirely logical, and laced with uncertainty. Ambiguities that would be fertile for learning are anathema to those who desire a well-run institution. The more the values, language, and activities of rational planning and management pervade the institution, the less time remains for the values, language, and activities that constitute significant learning.

* School systems are organized as "top-down" organizations. The problems of such organizations are well known. They tend to foster dependency in the middle and lower ranks. Instead of taking initiative, people waste time waiting for instructions. Since they have little say in the direction of the organization, they tend to become apathetic, which leads to poor use of time, or subversive, which means that time is spent "getting around the system." As these tendencies ripen in an organization, top-level managers try to "get around the workers" with more and more canned programs and mandates. Administrators adopt "teacher-proof" materials and textbooks that spell out minute-by-minute instructional activities. Teachers thus become "de-skilled," relying more and more on external expertise, less and less on their own craft knowledge, instincts, and training. Fewer and fewer questions get asked, fewer and fewer alternative choices appear, people take less and less responsibility for their work, passing the buck and sending problems up to the top where managers are so far away from them that they cannot come up with good solutions. Quality of instruction declines accordingly, and with it goes the quality of learning opportunities for students.

  Top-down administration historically has invited bottom-up resistance. It is not surprising that a workforce composed largely of women from blue-collar families would organize to bargain adversarially with an administrative workforce composed largely of men from white-collar backgrounds. But whatever the merits of an adversarial union/management arrangement, learning time for students is not enhanced when the adults around them are in bitter conflict, conducting work slow-downs or going out on strike. And the elaborate contracts that often emerge from bargaining add even more procedures, rules, regulations, meetings, and paperwork to a working environment already overloaded with them.

- Like so many mid-twentieth-century bureaucratic organizations, the school system atomizes the work to be done into hundreds of categories and subcategories, many of which require trained and certified "professionals" and specialists. Knowledge, already subdivided by subject areas, becomes further subdivided until all the king's horses and all the king's men could not put it back together again. Specialists in kindergarten play centers find they have little to say to specialists in phonics, who have little to say to third-grade whole language teachers, who do not converse with eighth-grade algebra teachers, who have nothing to say to Title 1 reading experts, who seldom meet with middle school art teachers, who seldom encounter tenth-grade counselors, who never see school nurses, who have nothing to say to school librarians, and so on. Each relatively isolated specialist is given, or develops, a curriculum that further fragments knowledge into little bits to be parceled out day by day in lesson plans. All of this fragmentation is a logical result of this particular form of organization. In the end, knowledge has been blown to smithereens and most students are left with a chaos that neither they, nor the adults around them, can shape into anything coherent enough to be useful. Moreover, the proliferation of specialists leads to departmental turf battles and redundancies that, again, consume time and energies that could be better employed.
- In short, the current organizational form of schooling guarantees that resources that could go into creating more powerful learning environments, go all too often, instead, into political squabbling, redundancy, reinvention of wheels, ineffective meetings, irresolvable disputes, band-aid solutions, cosmetic public relations, regulatory sadism, laborious grievance procedures, analyzing irrelevant information, deflection, subversion, circumvention, interdepartmental warfare, interest-group gridlock, passing the buck, shooting from the hip, and burning out.

Thus is precious time for student and adult learning squandered.

4

When my colleagues and I set out to do the studies of schooling that led to *Schools of Thought* (Brown, 1991), one of the hypotheses we wanted to test was this: Students will be no more literate or thoughtful than the adults around them in schools. In other words, if we expected to see students learning to use their minds fully, learning how to learn, we would be more likely to find them where teachers and other adults also were using their minds fully and learning right along with students. Conversely, where the adults were not visible and excited learners, we would not expect to find the students very involved in learning.

The hypothesis proved true far more often than not. This should not be a surprising finding. From their earliest moments, children learn from watching adults. Monkey see, monkey do. Time and again, when people describe their best teachers, they describe people passionately and visibly devoted to learning. It would make sense, then, to organize the enterprise of education in ways that encourage the adults to be learners in front of and along-side of young people. But the organization described above does not do this. It could even be argued that it is calculated to produce the opposite effect: adults who do not, and cannot, learn from each other, from students, or from the communities around them.

What kind of organization would be more appropriate? Observers have long noted the powerful learning that takes place in families, apprenticeships, residential schools, art colonies, and other settings that bring teachers and students together in intense, mutual learning experiences. Businesses recently have begun to acknowledge the limits of bureaucratic organization in fields demanding continuous learning. Studies of "cutting edge" busi-nesses here and abroad indicate that work environments that fos-ter group problem solving and group commitments to quality can markedly increase productivity. These considerations have given rise to models of "learning organizations" that might better suit the task of educating people than do bureaucracies, and might make better use of time for learning.

Education, reconceptualized in terms of a learning organiza-tion, would draw its organizational principles from what we know about learning. Tasks, roles, responsibilities, and resources would aim to stimulate and reinforce motivation, develop fluency in the language of instruction, and provide each individual with the time he or she needs to acquire foundational knowledge and process it thoroughly in various contexts for various purposes— that is, time to theorize, practice, and be exposed to many different opportunities to learn the knowledge in question; time to develop a certain kind of trust; time to understand and time to apply; time to read about it, write about it, discuss it, model it, make mistakes; time to compare new knowledge with primitive knowledge, schema, and theories; time to discover, inquire further, argue, and solve problems in novel situations. True equality of educational opportunity demands no less than this, *and* that there be no stigma attached to needing more time to learn any particular concept or subject.

Such an approach would yield a number of forms of organization that would share certain characteristics.

- They would have to be open to the communities around them, on the grounds that learning takes place 24 hours a day, and knowledge lies all about us, not just in formal learning institutions. This means that learning does not take place just in a school building. People are able to take advantage of learning opportunities wherever and whenever they occur. One such system for children is, of course, their families. We know that some child-rearing practices are more effective than others in helping kids learn informally and helping them bridge the gap between informal and formal learning. Children who are supported by parents, relatives, close adult friends, and siblings; who are encouraged to learn at home and rewarded for it; who are motivated by strong values and a sense of the future; who are given more time and appropriate space for formal learning at home; who teach one another in settings like Scouts or 4H Clubs; and who have continuing relationships with a variety of productive adults in their communities, learn more and learn faster than children who lack these opportunities. Daily experience is rich with opportunities to broaden children's knowledge and their capacities to process it, if there are adults around who know how to take advantage of such opportunities.

As numerous people have pointed out, the family provides the first learning environment for every child. The child who arrives at kindergarten with 14,000 hours of adult participation in his or her learning has an enormous head start on less fortunate children. Education's learning organization begins with the family, not the school building. Its success depends on having deep roots in families, strong relationships with families, clear, two-way communication with families, and participation of families. One would expect to see, in such organizations, parents in schools and teachers in homes; learning taking place in homes and parenting taking place in schools; arrangements for learning that range from 6 in the morning to 10 at night in varying settings; and a blurring of the distinctions between home and school.

Distinctions between school and neighborhood and community would blur, as well. Anyone can perform teaching tasks and facilitate learning, in the right circumstances, not just certified professionals. Many societies "manage" this kind of learning naturally through the agency of culture and social structures that bring children into regular contact with adults at work or play. Some communities and groups in the United States accomplish this naturally, as well. But many are dysfunctional in this regard. The first priority of an educational learning organization is to help rebuild such places until they are truly communities—that is, places where people routinely work together to define and solve the problems they face as citizens. The processes of building communities and creating learning organizations are similar in many respects. It makes sense for them to occur together, since people in a learning organization see themselves as *part of* their environment, not *apart from* it.

- Learning organizations would distribute planning widely, not centralize it. The point would not be for a few authorities to tell everyone else what to do, but, instead, for the system to foster conditions, under which people naturally learn from their experiences, accurately gauge what to do next, and do it. Teachers would not act out of some institutional mandate; they would act in response to what learners said they needed. Teachers' reference points would be students and their work, not bosses and their plans, textbooks and their teachers' guides, or unions and their work rules.

Only if planning is distributed widely can an organization serve diverse needs and respond quickly to social changes and unpredictable opportunities. IBM continued to focus resources on mainframe computers because that is what the organizational plan required. General Motors kept on doing what it had planned to do, as well, with the same result. During the year in which the Soviet empire collapsed, the vast majority of social studies teachers taught what the timed, planned curriculum required: facts about a world that even the students knew no longer existed. Because learning is a matter of opportunism, a learning organization must be structured to allow people to take advantage of every opportunity. Such an organization would have a vision about where, in general, it was headed; a set of ideas about how to get there; and processes for questioning and changing those ideas when they did not seem to work or when unforeseen opportunities cropped up. The people in such an organization would have to be good at scanning their environments, learning from their students and their own experiences, analyzing and interpreting information quickly, making decisions, shifting gears, and adapting to new circumstances. They also would have to know their subjects very, very well, in order to capitalize on events. People who can do only what they have been told to do cannot take advantage of learning opportunities and so would be at a serious disadvantage in a learning organization.

- Because of the above needs, a learning organization would distribute decision-making responsibilities widely and in ways that enabled the people closest to the problems and opportunities to deal with them effectively. The movement toward site-based management in Chicago, Los Angeles, and

Denver, represented an effort to decentralize decision making that had become bottled up in centralized bureaucracies. Experience shows that in the early stages, site-based, decision-making teams and school councils struggle. School boards are reluctant to relinquish power to make important decisions, and people unused to participating in the life of the school flounder in procedural disputes. But after several years, and given both training and the power to make significant decisions, they do begin to affect the learning environments of schools.

- Even the best school council cannot make good decisions if it lacks adequate information about what is going on in and around the school. The key to the learning organization would be maximum *knowledge flow*. The right kinds of data must be regularly gathered and made available to teams for interpretation, analysis, and what Gareth Morgan (1986), to whom I am greatly indebted for ideas about learning organizations, calls "inquiry-driven action" (p. 92). One of the greatest problems with the bureaucratic organization, as noted above, is that it fragments knowledge as it fragments responsibility and attention. Everyone becomes so concerned about his or her tiny domain that connections are lost and no one attends to the whole picture. We see the consequences in large school districts where English teachers try to make changes without regard for the needs of reading teachers, mathematics teachers try to reform mathematics instruction independently of science teachers, and bilingual teachers and Title 1 teachers operate with no reference to anyone else. Among them is a great reservoir of expertise, but it is unavailable to the system.

More problematic still is what happens to knowledge about each individual student. It is split up among numerous adults who do not talk to one another. No one has a picture of the whole child and his or her learning history. The abstractions teachers pass along from year to year—letter grades— are meaningless; the test scores that follow the student reveal only where she places in a national distribution of students, not what she knows. Students themselves throw away their papers and other evidence of learning as soon as they are graded, because they know no one will ever look at them again.

If schools were learning organizations, student work and student learning histories would be the most important knowledge to gather into wholes, interpret, and act upon. Key sources of knowledge critical for learning would include conversations with families about students, conversations among teachers about students, portfolios of student work, group inquiries into the meaning of student work, and conversations with community leaders about the relevance and quality of student work. The issue of quality would always be paramount, which means that values would always be visible, debatable, and changeable.

Since values are embedded in stories, as well as actions, a learning organization would provide opportunities for narrative as well as for critical analysis of narrative and action. All this does not mean there is no place for "hard data." It simply means that such abstract information cannot dominate the inquiry process and is always susceptible to an analysis of its underlying values and the limits they place on action.

- An educational learning organization would be structured and managed so that the adults were learners, along with the students. The learning organization requires a radically different form of management. As Morgan (1986) says, it must "root the process of organizing in a process of open-ended inquiry" (p. 91). This open-endedness is what enables the organization to respond to change and complexity in ways bureaucracies, with their predetermined ends, cannot. Group inquiry into problems also places much greater value on multiple perspectives, opening up decision making to a wider range of actors, distributing power relatively evenly, and bringing collective knowledge to bear on problems.

Managers in a learning organization would see their job not as telling others what to do but as facilitating knowledge flow and creating a culture and language of adult learning. They would spend time raising questions, facilitating discussions, and looking for emergent patterns in the discussion that might guide the group toward new forms of action. They

would be listeners, skilled at reframing issues so that they
could be approached in open-ended ways, experts at present-
ing problems systemically. They would be looking constantly
for ways to help people get the most out of their talents and
interests, and working constantly to find good fits between
tasks, the people doing them, and the ways they need to be
tackled. They would be the chief promoters of the spirits of
openness and trust and shared sense making necessary for
maximizing knowledge flow. They would call for, and
reward, creativity and innovation. They would look for and
share good stories that captured the vision of where the
organization was headed and the kinds of heroes it needed to
get there. They would call attention to themes and ideas that
were emerging from the group's activities. They would call
the group's attention to contradictions, without necessarily
trying to resolve them, knowing that some contradictions and
conflicts cannot and should not be resolved. They would
bring conversation back again and again to fundamental
questions of quality of work, quality of relationships, quality
of the discourse, quality and relevance of the norms and values that defined the limits of action.

Managers in a learning organization would see to it that
human and material resources were devoted to gathering the
right information, sharing it, analyzing it critically, and using
it to improve the learning process out of which action
emerges. They would provide other workers access to the
highest professional standards known, the best research, the
most helpful networks, and the most appropriate technologies. They would see to it that the organization, and each
group within it, had the variety of experiences, backgrounds,
and perspectives it needed to deal with the variety in its
clients and in the world around it. This means pushing constantly for diversity, not sameness; heterogeneity, not homo-
geneity; pluralism, not uniformity, on the grounds that the
organization cannot be efficient and responsive if it cannot
draw on many different talents and interests.

Managers in a learning organization spend most of their
time helping people think and learn—in other words, manage

themselves, according to a vision they share, information they have unearthed, standards they can create and change. They bring about more efficient use of time because they focus everyone on learning, not schooling.

5

It is bad enough that people in schools feel they do not have time to provide environments well known to promote learning. It is worse still that many of them do not believe they have the time to change their current mode of operation to something better. They are frozen in a form of inefficiency that prohibits any movement toward efficiency. So one of the most common questions they ask is, "How can I do all this new stuff and continue doing what I am already doing?"

Two short-term answers come to mind: stop doing what you are already doing; and do it in new ways that enable you to kill two or three birds with one stone. The long-term answer is to become a learning organization. But before schoolpeople take any course, they should find out what they are already doing. Most people have no idea how time is being used for learning in their buildings, in their students' homes, and in the communities around them.

The Carnegie Council on Adolescent Development provides an interesting starting point in *A Matter of Time: Risk and Opportunity in the Nonschool Hours* (1992). "By any standards," the Council writes, "America's young adolescents have a great deal of discretionary time. . . . Only 60 percent of adolescents' waking hours are committed to such essentials as school, homework, eating, chores, or paid employment" (p. 10). That means that the average young adolescent has about 45 hours per week—a full adult workweek and 130% of the time they spend in school—available for potential formal or informal learning experiences. For a quarter of the kids, 10–15 hours of that time are spent alone, after school. For most, half of the time is spent watching television.

Some young people do tap into the more than 17,000 youth programs available in communities across the country. Scouting, YMCA and YWCA programs, church programs, athletic leagues, museums, libraries, camps, and many other activities provide young people with structured learning opportunities that can reinforce or elaborate on what they do in school. Interaction with diverse peers in nonschool settings helps strengthen social skills necessary for collaborative learning. Interaction with adults, as noted earlier, provides endless modeling and mentoring possibilities, along with structure and safety. Many supervised youth activities and team sports require young people to plan, study, make decisions, read, write, communicate, do arithmetic, learn about the world of work, and solve problems.

Reginald Clark's (1988) research shows that when youth spend 20–35 hours a week engaged in "constructive learning activity," they are far more likely to be high achievers. Constructive learning activities include such things as discussion with knowledgeable adults, reading, writing, homework, hobbies, chores, games, theater, movies, museums trips, concerts, special events, and organized sports. Unproductive activities are passive and unchallenging at best, antisocial and self-destructive at worst. Rather than building children's resiliency—their sense of having some control over their environment, having a purpose and a future—unproductive activities make them still more vulnerable to forces that undermine their potential to learn and develop naturally.

Students who engage in these activities can have a significant learning advantage in school over those who do not. Students whose parents take them to interesting places like Epcot Center or Civil War battlefields, share a similar advantage, especially if the parents and young people talk, read, or write about their experiences. They are putting in more time learning. Unfortunately, research shows that the young people most likely to take advantage of these nonschool learning opportunities are the ones with greatest access to the widest range of programs: students from middle-class and affluent families.

No one is saying that young people should spend all their time in structured, supervised learning. Play is essential; a certain amount of time alone is important; time spent just "hanging out" or "goofing off" with friends is critical for healthy development. The evidence is clear, however, that more of that discretionary time and far more community resources can be brought to bear on learning than currently are. And for some students, that could make a major difference in their school achievement and life chances.

To be sure, the competition for that discretionary time is intense. As it has expanded, commercial marketing has moved in much faster than efforts to turn young people's time into learning opportunities. Teenagers now constitute an enormous economic force. Many teachers despair of competing successfully with the advertising glitter that both bedazzles young people and fragments their attention. It will not be easy to reclaim time for learning that is now spent on consumerism, but research indicates that many young people *want* to be more engaged in nonschool activities and significant work in their communities. "When the Task Force asked young adolescents what they wanted most during their nonschool hours," the Carnegie Council (1992) writes, "they replied: safe parks and recreation centers; exciting science museums; libraries with all the latest books, videos and records; trusting and trustworthy adults who know a lot about the world and who like young people; and opportunities to learn new skills" (p. 43).

The varying effects of economic forces on neighborhoods create varying opportunities for structured, supervised youth activities. Outer suburbs, consisting of sprawling housing tracts, punctuated by malls, offer little that young people can pursue without parents willing and able to drive them long distances. Tract planning seems to rest on the assumption that all the necessary cultural resources are in each family's home and that suburbanites prefer their "lifestyle enclaves," as Bellah, Madsen, Sullivan, Swidler, and Tipton (1985) called them, to a strong sense of community. Established suburbs closer to a city, and affluent metropolitan neighborhoods, offer more access per child than anyplace else to a greater range of organized activities.

Poor urban neighborhoods can be as culturally impoverished as outer suburbs and, on top of that, lack the family resources available to suburban children. Poor urban neighborhoods tend to have sub-par public facilities, more danger for young people with time on their hands, fewer youth development programs and services, fewer positive adult models for children to interact with, and, as a frequent consequence, gang activities, rather than more constructive outlets for ingenuity. Again, competition for discretionary time that has been captured, in the inner city, by *both* consumerism and gang activities, can make recapturing time for learning very difficult, but it is far from impossible.

These variations in the availability of formal youth development opportunities suggest that each community must make its own assessment of its nonschool learning resources. The evidence is that wherever there are caring adults and networks to link them with other adults and resources across neighborhoods and communities, *and wherever a coherent community youth policy provides support and direction for collaboration*, opportunities for nonschool learning abound. The first job for educators is to work with community-based organizations to audit, connect, and strengthen learning opportunities throughout the community, because they offer the greatest untapped reservoir of non-school time available for learning and learning how to learn.

The questions for educators in any school are:

- what are the family and community resources available for helping our students learn outside of school?
- how good are they, that is, how well do the adults provide learning opportunities and reinforce learning?
- how much time is each student devoting to these nonschool learning opportunities?
- how do we build on each student's nonschool learning experiences and connect them to school learning?

This information could be gathered, analyzed, and presented by students themselves. Some of it could be gathered over the summer through mail surveys of parents and community leaders. Regular "summits" of educators and leaders of other youth-serving organizations could lead to a "learning resources guidebook" for students and parents and to adult training to improve the capacities of youth organizations to capitalize on potential cognitive learning opportunities, as well as opportunities for social, physical, emotional, and moral development.

How can people make better use of time in schools? First, they have to meet some *threshold conditions*. Studies of school reform and restructuring show that in certain circumstances, schoolpeople find the time they need to improve, and in other circumstances, they do not. Favorable circumstances include:

- agreement among a majority of staff members that reform is necessary and there will be clear benefits to them and to their students as they move ahead;
- general agreement about the principles undergirding the reforms and the change process they will be going through;
- leadership that supports change, establishes clear priorities, and helps find the time;
- some freedom to maneuver, gained through waivers and variances, if necessary;
- "mad money," from private sources or a district reform stimulus fund, to buy time and substitutes;
- active membership in a network of schools going through a similar process;
- staff development in holding efficient and productive meetings, collaboration, conflict resolution, creativity, and the change process;
- community and parental support;
- reform-oriented policies in place that reinforce change and provide guidance.

In schools where most of these conditions exist, people tend to find the time. In schools where people lack agreement, don't talk much or well to each other, lack leadership, feel no freedom to take risks, feel isolated and embattled, lack community support, and experience interference and resistance from central administration, people tend not to be able to find the time. A few teachers here and there, inspired by their professional associations, take time-out of their families' lives to mount heroic reform efforts alone or in little clusters. But they tend to tire after 4 or 5 years and they have no long-term effect on the school at large.

Another thing schoolpeople can do is *find out how time is currently used*. Most people do not know. The first step toward finding out is to define *productive* learning time (which leads to understanding and ability to apply what is learned in new contexts) and discuss thoroughly how it looks and sounds. This should be done in faculty meetings, in meetings of the school reform team or council, in classrooms, and in community meetings that are already taking place. Staff could begin by committing one-third of the usual time for a meeting and one-tenth of the usual classroom period to this discussion. They should encourage people to introduce into the discussion examples of student work that reflect degrees of learning, to argue about its quality, and to develop categories and scales of quality.

It may happen that what emerges from the discussion is not a single definition of productive learning but several types of learning, all of which staff may want to monitor. When groups have reached some agreement about categories and signs of learning activities, they can design, with students, a School Time Study. The first version of the time audit need not be very sophisticated. Its purpose is to provide a general profile of time uses in broad categories. It might be helpful to focus on time spent reading, writing, thinking critically, thinking creatively, and solving problems, alone or with others. The data can be gathered with pencil and paper or with videotape.

In the classroom, some key categories include time spent on:

- teacher lecturing, giving directions, disciplinary comments
- questioning and probing (teacher and students)
- representing concepts in several forms (e.g., graphs, tables, algebraic notation, sentences, models, drawings, dance, etc.)
- reading (for pleasure, for solving problems, for quick recall, for comprehension)
- writing (for pleasure, for solving problems, note taking, in different subjects, rewriting)
- discussion (with reasons for point of view, respectful listening, acceptance of alternative points of view)
- recitation, drill, rote learning
- collaborative learning groups

- seminars (e.g., Great Books discussions, Socratic seminars)
- student presentations
- seatwork
- tutoring
- testing, test preparation
- laboratory work, experimentation
- making things, projects, models
- doing nothing
- listening to announcements over the public address system

Teachers also can log their uses of nonclassroom time (e.g., cafeteria duty, hall monitoring, counseling, meeting, planning, disciplining, correcting papers, and scoring tests) during and after regular school hours. Administrators can do the same (out-of-building time, phone time, paperwork, discipline, etc.). So, of course, can individual students, librarians, nurses, Special Education teachers, and anyone else working in the school. The point is to discover how time is being spent currently in order to look for new efficiencies and to establish a baseline against which to measure progress.

If a staff agrees that major goals of teaching are to create rich knowledge connections; help students to remember, understand, and apply their knowledge; and teach each student how to continue learning throughout his or her life, it can begin to define "efficiency" and "inefficiency." Inefficient learning experiences may be defined, for example, as lessons that provide no contexts for the learning and no connections between the lesson and other lessons, facts, or experiences. Inefficient teaching may be teaching that helps only a few students, that offers only one or two ways of accessing or processing knowledge, or that relegates students to passive roles in their learning. Any particular lecture might be more or less efficient in the ways it organizes, presents, and connects knowledge to the lives of the listeners; but even good lecturing may be inefficient compared with other forms of pedagogy that engage students more directly and deeply in learning experiences.

A staff may want to define characteristics of efficient learning, that is, how you know it when you see it. One characteristic, for instance, might be that what was learned can be expressed in a number of ways, can be written about extensively, and can be applied in contexts other than the one in which it was learned. Working backwards, if a student cannot remember much from a learning experience, the learning experience probably was not efficient; likewise, if the student cannot elaborate on the new knowledge, connect it to other kinds of knowledge, or use it in different ways and contexts, it probably was not efficient.

Staff may want to create a ratio between time and amount learned, in order to define some aspect of efficiency. If a teacher and 24 students spend 10 hours on a particular concept, for instance, they have invested 250 person-hours in learning. What might we reasonably expect from such an investment? One answer might be that the teacher learned nothing (she already knew the concept) and the 24 students all learned the same concept and could express what they learned in the same way. Another answer might be that the 24 students learned the concept in different ways, which they shared with one another, thus squaring the amount of information available for thorough learning and, in the process, teaching the teacher something she hadn't thought of before.

Defining efficiency is not easy. The education system historically has bypassed measures of learning efficiency, choosing, instead, traditional bureaucratic measures of institutional efficiency: dollars per pupil, dropout rate, percentage of students going on to college, and test score averages. By describing performance in terms of bell-shaped curves, averages, and norms, the system has not just evaded questions of real efficiency, but rendered them unaskable. Not knowing what their potential is, individual students have no way of knowing whether they are learning at 50% of potential or 10%. Not knowing what knowledge and skills students already possess when they enter school, educators do not know what value they have added to their clients. Not knowing how much could be learned in 10 weeks—indeed, protected from knowing by the timed curriculum—teachers have no way of knowing whether instruction is wasteful or productive. But however difficult it may be to come up with measures of learning efficiency, it is important for people to try. Real professionals are concerned with quality; and quality inheres as much in the habit of trying to define it as in the practice of acting on what the group has decided, so far in the quest, it is.

A staff could define an ideally efficient lesson by which to analyze and evaluate current practice. It could say, for instance, that by definition the most efficient action produces the most effects. The ideally efficient lesson for a group of 25 students, therefore, would provide or draw on the motivation of all 25; would draw on and extend the foundational knowledge of all 25; would draw on, increase, or reinforce the learning process knowledge of all 25; would enable all students to place the new knowledge in personal and social contexts that give it meaning and help them remember it; would provide opportunities for the knowledge to be approached from all possible theoretical, practical, and cultural points of view; would involve reading, writing, mathematics, and the arts as languages by which to represent, express, and manipulate the knowledge; would place the burden of thinking critically, inquiring, thinking creatively, reflecting, and solving problems squarely on the backs of the students; would force students to compare their new formal knowledge with their old informal, primitive knowledge; would provide opportunities for students to model, perform, and exhibit what they have learned; would take advantage of knowledge networks in and around the school, including the students themselves, their parents, and community resources; would provide feedback to all about the quality of the learning experience and opportunities for all to consider ways of raising the quality of the experience; would connect to past and future lessons in and across subject disciplines; and would build confidence, self-esteem, and a devotion to learning among all concerned. With such a standard in mind, teachers could begin to analyze current lesson plans and units of study during their planning periods, team meetings, and inservice workshops.

Schoolpeople also can find better ways of using time within the current model of schooling. Susanna Purnell and Paul Hill, in their monograph "Time for Reform" (1992), found that teachers involved in reform have found six ways of creating extra time. The one most often used is freeing teachers from classroom duties so they can go to workshops, observe other teachers, or observe other schools. To cover the teachers' time, schools use substitutes, university faculty and students, outside speakers, parents, and community volunteers. Such rotations can be doubly efficient if, after a while, the people substituting for the teachers develop instructional or noninstructional skills that complement the missing teacher's. Teachers also can draw on other staff inside the building: administrators can substitute and other teachers can take double classes, while some plan or train or analyze student work.

A second option is to change the nature of staff meetings so that they focus more on reform issues than on the usual logistical and political concerns. Teachers also could bargain for a contract with more staff development days in it or seek grants for summer work.

A third approach noted by Purnell and Hill is changing the school schedule so that teachers have more time for working together. Teams can be assigned the same planning periods; periods can be "blocked" into longer units, freeing up certain teachers on certain days; 10 minutes of homeroom can be eliminated each day and "banked" until an extra hour is created for teacher learning; students can be released early or come in late one day a week, freeing up an afternoon or morning for planning and staff development.

A fourth way to create time is to add time to the workweek or year through supplemental contracts, special stipends, additional contract days, and days paid for by foundation grants. A fifth is to create rewards and incentives for teachers to use their free time in ways that move reform ahead. They may earn recertification credits, for example, or credits toward sabbaticals or extra vacation days. And finally, teachers can try to take advantage of technology to connect them to staff development activities or to reduce the time they spend on paperwork, drills, and other activities that can be assigned to computers.

The most important, and most neglected, approach to finding time for reform is to turn more responsibility for learning over to students. Often one student can motivate another more easily than an adult can. Students can be excellent tutors of other students, given the right training and support. And tutors needn't be the high achievers; many a mediocre student, given the responsibility to help a younger student, learns more about a subject or about literacy skills as "teacher" than he or she did as "student." Cooperative learning teams, with the right questions to pursue, the right materials and training, can be extremely efficient ways to let learning happen among students, while teachers circulate and provide individualized help. Peer editing has been shown to be a very effective way to teach students how to spot and correct their own writing weaknesses, as well as those of others.

Students can take responsibility for teaching units or parts of units; they can lead discussions, play devil's advocate, create essay questions and scoring protocols, conduct research, contact community experts and bring them into the classroom, do maintenance work in the school, run the cafeteria, create and run businesses, create school security systems, staff the computer lab, create and run a school court for disciplinary procedures, take charge of entertainment, create formal study groups, and do any number of things now being done by adults. Students did all of these things in P.S. 1, and I have visited a number of other schools where they do them as well. It helps if the schools are small. Then, it is all a matter of setting expectations for students from the moment they enter the school and giving them significant responsibilities and the training they need to carry them out with confidence.

Besides being good learning experiences, student-led activities have the added virtue of freeing up teacher time for professional development. The fact is that teachers need not be in front of classrooms all day, 5 days a week. They do not do so in other countries and they do not do so in higher education. The more responsibility for learning we turn over to students, the more time we free up for their teachers to learn what they need to know in order to create the kinds of learning environments that are much more efficient and productive than the ones that predominate today.

6

Most schools have not yet taken advantage of all the opportunities for improving efficiency that lie before them, even within the current organizational structures that define their uses of time. Much can be done to improve learning opportunities and enrich learning experiences before educators have "maxed out" the possibilities for better use of time in the average school. The key is great leadership. But one of the ironies of the current system is that although great leadership can bring about significant improvements, the system provides few incentives for greatness of any kind and is not professionally appealing to the people who might provide the necessary leadership. So in the last analysis, our current approach to schooling places a glass ceiling on what can be accomplished. Breakthroughs in the uses of time for genuine learning will require fundamental changes in the organization of learning experiences inside and outside schools, across communities, and in the world of work.

This cannot happen on any large scale until policies that overdetermine the present uses of time are changed. Current interest in moving to outcomes rather than Carnegie units, performance rather than seat time, represents a necessary step in the right direction. The current realization that the entire system must change, not just elements of it, is on the mark. Whether we have the political courage to follow through on such a bold vision, remains to be seen.

CHAPTER 4

It's Your Fault!

1

When you're the principal of an urban middle school/high school, you have to keep your emotions in check. You have to keep your cool. You can't act like the kids. You have to be considerate and thoughtful, biting your tongue until it bleeds. But what would you say if, just once, you could cave in to the temptation to let it all out like the kids do? This is what it might sound like:

Parents, it's your fault!

These are your kids, after all. You supposedly "raised" them, and you have them 90% of the time. The apple doesn't fall far from the tree.

Where do you get off blaming the *schools* for anything? You're lucky teachers are sappy enough to look after your kid while you're traipsing all over God knows where. Here it is, 6 o'clock at night, and you still haven't shown up to take your kid home and he's clinging to the teacher's leg like it's the mast of a ship that's going down! I'm talking to you, Ms. Big shot lawyer who always has to work late because your work's so *important*. With all your education and all your money, you haven't got the faintest idea how to nurture a child. I'll bet this kid was started right out on formula. Am I right? He's got that formula kind of look around the eyes.

When's the last time you had a good talk with this boy? He's got that nobody talks to me look, too. What's the national average amount of time families like yours are spending talking to their kids? Five minutes a week? Four? What happens in the summer? Nanny? Solange, the *au pair*? Or does he go to Computer Camp? Or is he a "big boy" who can stay home alone all day watching television and feeding the pets, who, if it weren't for him, would probably die, and watering the plants, which, because of him, are dying of overwatering.

Stop sniggering, dad. You wouldn't think of watering the plants, would you? Or talking to your kid about anything substantive or even being around much, except when Solange is there, and even then you spend all your time talking with her and sucking in your gut. Mr. Disciplinarian. "Give him what-for if he gets out of line," you say on your way out the door on the days it's your turn to pick up the kid late. Don't worry. He's going to get out of line. He's going to send you some little messages about getting out of line when he's a teenager. You can count on him getting your attention some day, some way. He's got that look around the eyes.

You middle-class parents with your "gifted" kids. Who are you kidding? Not anyone at this school. We know that little Nellie's sharp as a pin in some areas and stupid as a post in others. How did you wangle that "gifted" classification? Did you happen to threaten to pull her out of the public schools if she wasn't declared "gifted"? Look, we know the story. Your two best friends' children are in "gifted" classes at their schools and you'll lose face if your kids aren't geniuses, too. So you kept badgering everyone about how underchallenged she was and how all those ungifted kids and out-of-control kids in regular classrooms were holding her back. The squeaky wheel gets the grease, and you sure know how to squeak. You wore somebody down.

Aren't you the one who said the school ought to offer advanced algebra in seventh grade? The one who argued that if we didn't do that, students like your daughter would not be able to take geometry in eighth grade, and if they couldn't get through geometry in eighth grade, they couldn't get into accelerated classes in high school, and if they couldn't get into accelerated classes they would never get admitted into Ivy League colleges? You're really hysterical about this, aren't you? You really think that little Nellie's life is hanging in the balance. And look at her! She's a *sixth grader*. She's, like, *3 feet tall*!

"Helicopter moms" (you know, the ones who hover over their children all the time): How about giving your kids a little room to breathe? There's a difference between mothering and smothering. Will you leave that kid alone, for crying out loud? Look at him! Look how embarrassed he is when you keep coming in here to correct all his mistakes. He's a *kid*. He's *supposed* to make mistakes. That's how he *learns*. Remember the time we suspended him along with four other guys because they all made the same bad decision? And you said if I didn't erase his suspension, you'd sue the school? Did you really think you were doing him a *favor*? He said, "Mom, I did it and I should be suspended for it," and you told him he didn't know what he was talking about. You told him that the suspension would keep him out of the international baccalaureate program, and he said—*he* said—"I guess I should have thought of that." And you didn't even hear him. You went back to trying to break my chops. Go ahead. Sue the school into bankruptcy.

What is wrong with you people out there? Didn't anyone tell you *anything* about parenting? Where are your priorities? Have you noticed that your kid is drawing pistols and machine guns and explosions all over his notebooks? What's *that* about? Weren't you the one who worried that our school might have too many violence-prone city kids in it for your little suburban angel? Hello? In case you haven't noticed, the massacres are out in the suburbs.

Not that city people can't be just as obnoxious as pushy WASPs. Yeah, I'm talking about you, sister, the shrill, self-appointed avenger of racism. Can't start the day without eating a White man for breakfast. Little Jamal flunks a spelling test? Spelling tests are racist. He mouths off at the teacher? The teacher is a racist. He hits somebody? He's *supposed* to stick up for himself, and, anyway, the other kid made a racist remark. I suspend him? I'm a racist. The system backs me up? The system's racist. Life's real simple for you, isn't it? Everybody's out to get your son or daughter. They don't have to take responsibility for anything, do they? No matter what they do, they were provoked, and no matter what the verdict on their behavior, it won't be fair.

Ah, the joys of self-righteousness, of victimhood, of self-pity! Oh, the satisfaction of screaming your lungs out at some underpaid, harried grunt who's trying to keep your kid from destroying himself or someone else. Why don't you spend less time looking for insults and more time looking for something constructive to do? Why don't you get on with your life? Are you planning to stay stuck here in your anger and bitterness forever? I'll tell you this: I've had it with you coming to meetings and blowing them up like a suicide bomber. Just when we get some positive energy going and people are beginning to feel they can do something, you come in on cue and bring everybody down with your yelling or your crying or your corrosive, cynical suspicion. It's obvious to everyone that you're miserable and you don't want us to go home until we feel worse than you do.

Look, grandpa: Ten people saw your granddaughter throw a big rock through the van window and you're telling me she was framed by a White teacher who hates Mexicans and, anyway, other kids—White kids—were throwing rocks into the creek and they aren't being punished and you knew she was going to be treated like crap because she always has been and you always have been and your ancestors always have been, just because you're all Mexicans. I'm not going to ask why you, not her parents, are raising her, although I happen to know that her parents—your children—are junkies and her father is doing hard time. She's a monster, this granddaughter of yours, a holy terror, and everybody knows it. You've made a mess of things. We have plenty of Mexican kids at this school whose families have faced treatment you can't even imagine, and they're good kids. They don't feel like victims and they don't act like victims and their families don't make excuses. Learn from them. Get over it.

All of you parents, rich and poor, let's get something straight. My teachers are here for your kids, day and night. They're busting their picks. You, meanwhile, are the ones who give your jobs priority over your kids, who get divorces, who get drunk every night, who scream and yell at each other over nothing, who sleep around, who beat each other and your kids, who move the kids from school to school until they can't trust anyone, who don't have dinner with them, who don't converse with them, who don't read with them, who don't help them with their homework, who let them watch anything they want, who let them stay up till all hours, who let them get their own breakfasts and make their own lunches and trudge out to the bus stop in the dark and trudge home in the dark to an empty house.

This isn't rocket science: Children who experience high levels of stress and sickness and trauma at home tend to develop high levels of depression, anxiety, and anger, which conditions interfere with their abilities to trust, hope, empathize, focus, and take initiative, which conditions in turn interfere with their abilities to learn as quickly and easily as kids who do not have these burdens. Kids in families where no one talks about anything substantive, where adults don't explore the world much with their kids, where no one reads or writes, where there is no give and take, where there are no opportunities to develop internal controls on their behavior because all control is external and coercive, do not learn as quickly or as easily as other kids. Nor do they fit in, socially, which further aggravates their problems learning. Children who aren't loved in a healthy adult way don't learn to love in a healthy adult way, and that, too, makes them worse students than they otherwise would be. "Failing schools" my ass; it's failing families that are killing us, and you know it.

Whose fault is that? I'm just getting started. But you don't get off the hook by pointing your finger at "poverty" or "society" or "capitalism" or "the man." Your child is standing there right now, peering up at you. You're obligated to act on what everyone knows about learning *right now*, not after some revolution. Return his gaze. Notice the look around the eyes. Say something new.

2

Students, it's your fault!

You lying, thieving, conniving, manipulative little mollusk: I know you did it. I can see right through that angelic look of yours. There's a full-grown criminal in that skinny little 11-year-old body. Everyone can see it but your mother, poor thing. Here she is, risking her day job by coming into school to bawl me out. She believes your cock and bull stories. You've got her wrapped around your finger. Now you're going to pull out the tears, the "I didn't do it!"

sobs, you little weasel. And all the other tools of deception, distraction, and deflection: "nobody told me" (somebody told you), "I didn't hear the teacher" (you heard), "so-and-so did it first and he's not being punished" (tough luck; I'll get him next), "that stupid teacher has it in for me, he doesn't give me any work to do, I try to ask him questions but he never answers them, he yelled at me, he grabbed me, he hates me, he said I was stupid, I never went near his desk, honest, I found it, I don't know how it got in my pocket, honest, why would I lie?" You'd lie because you're a kid and you all lie when you're cornered.

Look, just admit stuff and move on. You aren't morally formed yet, you did something impulsive and got caught, it happens all the time. Pay the price, try to learn from it and move on. Stop wasting all this time trying to convince me that you're more morally advanced than I was when I was your age. You're a kid, you make mistakes, we catch you, we show you the error of your ways. Eventually, you get to do the same thing when you're grown up.

Hey Mr. slob, I've got a news flash for you: This school isn't your pigsty of a room at home. Stop spitting your gum onto the carpet and spilling your Dr. Pepper on the computer and putting your boogers on the door knobs and throwing staplers in the toilets and writing over everything in the room with your leaky ballpoint pen. And the graffiti! What's with that? You little wolverine. We busted our picks raising the money it took to give you a pleasant place to learn, and you just crap all over it. I'm coming over to your house tonight, armed with spray paint, a dead skunk, and a couple of bags of pig manure. I'm going to make your room suitable for an animal like you.

You guys are such cons. The whining, the wheedling, the sucking up, the slacking—we see it all. You're not getting away with anything. You know how you slip down in your chair and put your head on your desk behind the kid in front of you so you can sleep, thinking that no one can see you? Who do you think you are? The Invisible Man? Don't you realize that anyone standing in front of the class—EVEN A DWARF—sees *everything*? Do you really believe that if *you* can't see me, *I* can't see you? With your legs splayed out into the aisle and your gorilla arms hanging down to the floor and your hair sticking out all over the place? I see you, all right. I've got nice snapshots of you collapsed on your desk, one for your parents, one for you, and one for my Slacker Hall of Fame. I'd go easy on you if I thought you were getting up with the sun to milk the cows or something, but I know you're tired because you stayed up most of the night watching something *totally stupid* on television.

We have a disconnect here. I'm trying to help you learn things that everyone thinks you should know and you don't give a hoot in hell. I'm even trying to help you learn things that *you* want to know and I can't get anywhere. I asked you the other day, "What are you interested in?" And you said, "I dunno." You *must* know! There must be *something*! It wasn't a trick question. *Any* answer will do—girls, food, skateboarding. I don't care. Just give me SOME-THING TO WORK WITH HERE. "I dunno." "What was the question?" I asked you what you're curious about, what questions you might have about anything. "Nuthin." You're interested in nothing? You're not curious about *anything*? Is this because *you already know everything there is to know about everything*? I DON'T THINK SO! If you already know everything, how come the only thing you ever say is, "I dunno"?

How about this: I'll make a statement and you respond with an opinion. Okay? "I dunno." Here's the statement: "All teenagers should be rounded up and imprisoned until they are 25 years of age. Your opinion?" "I dunno." What do you mean you don't know? Do you want me to throw you in prison *right now*? "I guess not." You *guess* not? Why not just say NO? "I dunno." Okay, never mind; we're getting somewhere. Why would you guess not? "Cause it wouldn't be fair." AHA! A reason! And why wouldn't it be fair? "It just wouldn't be." Why wouldn't it be? "I dunno." But you must have some idea about what fairness is, right? Some opinion? Or you could not have used the word in a sentence. Tell me, why would it be unfair if I imprisoned you right here, right now? "Cause I didn't do nuthin." Are you kidding? You're driving me crazy! That's reason enough for *me* to throw you in prison. Why isn't it reason enough for you? "I dunno." What would it take for me to convince you that it was fair of me to throw you into prison—no, to throw you into a pit of vipers? "That it was good for me, not just you." So fairness has something to do with more than one person thinking it was fair? And it has something to do with what is good or bad for people? Does anyone else in the class agree with Mr. Jordan about the nature of justice? Missy? "The bell rang, Mr. Brown." Aaarghhh.

Day after day of this. It's like pulling teeth out of a hippopotamus. The resistance! The stonewalling! The refusal to entertain even the tiniest thought! No, it's worse than that. It's a refusal to *even enter into a conversation* with an adult. Do you know how maddening that is? It's like potty training an intellectual retentive who'd rather *wet his pants* than give me one jot of influence over his little *will*.

Let's face it: It's a battle to the finish, day in and day out. You don't like grown-ups. They have all the power. It's not fair. You don't want to grow up. It doesn't look like any fun, anyway. And we don't like you. You're *unformed*. You're *incomplete*. You're *manipulative*. You gang up on us, 30 or 40 of you in a room, massed against the only adult, ready to stick up for one another against the teacher at the drop of a pencil, ready to unleash all the pent-up anger and resentment of childhood as soon as some poor, sentimental schmoo of a teacher drops her guard or turns her back on you. And if we try to do anything about it? "It's not FAIR!" you'll scream. "It's not RIGHT!"

Let's get something else straight, while we're being honest: You're ignorant. That's why you're here. You don't know much. You haven't lived long enough to know much. You have a lot to learn. I'm sick and tired of you acting as if you know what you're talking about when you don't. "The government is killing everyone," you say in social studies. And when Mr. Rushton asks you to name one person the government has killed, you clam up and say, "I know what I know." Why don't you just say, "I feel what I feel," and avoid the embarrassment of never having any evidence for anything you supposedly "know"? We'll all grant that you have feelings galore, but feelings aren't knowledge.

Also, you're narcissistic, totally self-involved. This, too, comes with your age. Remember when we were talking about *Moby Dick* and you said it was a stupid book because "if a whale bit my leg off, I wouldn't go chasing after it?" The book wasn't about you. It was about somebody else who *would* chase a whale that bit his leg off. You're supposed to imagine what that would be like. But how can you imagine what characters are like in books when you can't even imagine *another human being besides yourself*? Hello? There are 6 billion of us out here, outside of your thick skull. We're not you. We're not extensions of your will. We're OTHERS. Sooner or later you will have to come to grips with this. I'd rather it were sooner. You're getting on my nerves.

3

Teachers, it's your fault!

What kind of phony baloney "profession" is this, anyway? Doctors, lawyers, architects—those are professionals. They work as long as it takes to get the job done. What kind of doctor would tell you he can't operate after hours because it's "against the contract"? What kind of lawyer leaves the building at 2:30 because it's "in the contract"? *What kind of professional goes on strike?* Face it: You've got more in common with dockworkers than professionals. You-all and your work rules.

Please, please, stop the whining about your lot. It's a tough job, all right, but there are tougher ones in the world. And almost everyone with a college degree has long since figured out how to improve working conditions and pay without turning to Jimmy Hoffa. Your union has this system tied up in knots. You're spending too much time wrestling with moronic administrators and crazy school boards, lobbying for useless legislation, protecting bad teachers, and flattering presidential candidates. It's all time and energy you could better use learning how to do your job well. You need this union like you need a hole in the head. You think it's keeping you alive, but it's killing you.

Remember the last strike? Remember how you stopped talking to your best friend because he wanted to keep teaching? And when the strike was over, you taught in the classroom next to his for 4 years and still never talked to him. Was it worth it? Do you tell your students to act like that? Remember how you're always talking about how little respect teachers get? Do you suppose your union's behavior might have something to do with that?

Actually, you get more respect than politicians, lawyers, and businesspeople. We all have stories about a teacher who turned our lives around or told us we had talent or just liked us, when no one else did. After all, as they're growing up, kids get to see at least 50 teachers for every doctor or lawyer who might come into their lives. The teaching practice has a real PR advantage over any other practice or profession. Everything people come to know about teaching and learning, they absorb from that vast sample of practitioners and their thousands and thousands of hours listening to them droning on and on and on. Public opinion about teachers isn't based on snap judgments; it's hard won. You taught them how to think about you. Nobody else did. So if substantial numbers of people grow up to see teachers as whiners and victims, they must have encountered a substantial number of whiners and victims in school. If they see teachers as drones who carry out someone else's agenda, it's because they saw a lot of drones in school carrying out someone else's agenda instead of thinking for themselves. If they have come to believe that teaching is no fun, it's because they've seen substantial numbers of crabby teachers, toughing it out until retirement. If they think teachers are bossy and mean, it's because they've seen a lot of bossy and mean teachers.

Not you, of course, Mr. or Ms. "alternative educator." You're in it "just for the kids," right? You're not bossy or mean, you're their *friend*. They call you by your first name; they brush your hair and hang out at your house. Your classroom is about "feeling safe and nurtured." God forbid they should learn how to spell or count or do anything they don't want to do. Who are you to impose rules on them or to make them conform to the dictates of this "sick" society? Who are you to say anything is better than anything else or that learning this is better than learning that? Better they grow up ignorant than grow up bourgeois. Better yet that they not grow up at all, like you. I know your type: far more comfortable with children than with adults. You say it's because children are naturally good, whereas adults are naturally bad. I say it's because you still feel like a child and you're terrified of adults and all the responsibilities they have to shoulder. You're developmentally stuck and you found a job that makes it easy to stay stuck.

All of you: Here's what your job boils down to: monkey see, monkey do. If you want kids to be learners, you have to be a learner. If you want them to ask good questions, you have to ask good questions. If you want them to take risks, you have to take risks. If you expect them to make mistakes, expect yourself to make mistakes. If you want them to love reading, you should love reading. If you want them to write, you should write. If you want them to be curious, you should be curious. If you want them to grow up, you should grow up. Got it?

You don't have a prayer if you're a know-it-all or if you're pretending to be a know-it-all because you're terrified they'll find out you don't know it all. "Find out?" They already know! They've got the Internet at home or just down the hall, and they've got television sets. You can't compete with those. Knowledge and two bucks will get you a cup of coffee. It's not about knowledge anymore. It's about what are they going to do with all this knowledge that's coming down on them like an avalanche? You'll have to be somebody else, like just a regular human being who's trying to figure things out and can help them do it, too. The knowledge thing is *over*. The Mr. Wizard thing is *over*. Stop standing in front of them like some sort of professor; sit in the middle. Say things like, "I wonder," or "I don't get it," or "what the heck is going on?" or "I'm not sure," or "I haven't the faintest idea—let's find out!" Ask them what they think and why they think that.

Don't be so afraid of questions. If you've taught them how they can check up on you, it won't make any difference if you guess at answers or say something that's flat wrong. You can bring it up tomorrow and talk about why you thought you knew the answer and how you misled yourself and how they might mislead themselves if they commit the same thinking mistakes. Stop hiding all your thinking and pretending that you acquired your wisdom in a flash of insight. Show them how you were ignorant once, just like them, and you learned everything the hard way, getting it wrong, and then getting it partly right and partly wrong, and then making big mistakes with it, and finally getting to where you are now: more informed, better able to think things through, chastened by all your stupidities, confident about some of your knowledge but still open to the possibility that you could be wrong or you could have lots more to learn.

How can you teach this curriculum with a straight face? Look at it: It lays out the laws of math and science as if Moses brought them from the mountain, all nice and tidy. No hint that some poor schnook went mad trying to prove a theorem or some Arab figured something out 1,200 years ago and then the whole world forgot it for 700 years, or a hundred thousand people worked on the problem over 200 years until it could be explained in one paragraph in some textbook. All the sweat and tears, all the hard thinking, all the red herrings, all the experiments that went awry and all the hypotheses that bombed are gone. All that remains is a "law of nature," purified of human contact, stripped of historical context, irrelevant to kids, sitting there in the textbook to be memorized for no apparent reason. And you buy into it uncritically and pass it on to the kids and wonder why they aren't interested. They aren't interested, just to push the point, *because everything remotely interesting about how human beings came to discover the phenomena that came to be known as "laws" has been hidden from them.*

The way things are presented to kids is not the way they were learned by real people in real time. Your job is to demystify knowledge by showing kids where it really comes from, how it really evolves. Knowledge is a product of thinking; different knowledge bases are the products of different kinds of thinking. Students need to experience and understand their own thinking and learn how to evaluate it; then they need to experience and understand and evaluate other people's thinking. That's the core of your job: Think, think when you're planning what to do, think while you're doing it right in front of kids, make them think, make them evaluate their thinking. Let them experience what everyone who has made a contribution to human knowledge has experienced: the joys and frustrations of thinking, of discovering, of saying "Aha!" or "Oh no!" or "Eureka!" If you can't or won't do that, you're probably in the wrong job and you're certainly not a professional. Professionals think and reach independent judgments.

English teachers: Will you stop it with the grammar? Eighty years of research shows that teaching grammar is not teaching writing. You teach them grammar for 12 years, for crying out loud, and they hate every minute of it and remember nothing. *They learned the whole language as toddlers without a single grammar lesson!* They learn to write by writing, not by studying linguistics. They learn to edit by editing. They learn the sound and rhythm of good writing by reading good writing. But look at what you're doing: You're not asking them to write much more than the homework assignments on the blackboard and you're not asking them to read much more than those terribly written, "vocabulary controlled" textbooks that you won't even let them take home for fear that they'll read ahead! Where's your common sense? And when you ask them to write, it's about something in which they're not remotely interested. They dash something off and you read it with zero interest. No real reason for writing and no real reason for reading, except that both of you "have to." They hate writing for you and you hate reading their drivel. Is it any wonder that you fall asleep reading their totally predictable and boring papers about *Romeo and Juliet*? You've set yourself up, man. You've doomed yourself to reading stuff from which you can't learn any-thing—which is why it's so boring—because *you wrote the assign-ment in such a way that they had to bore you in order to "do well."*

"These inner-city kids aren't interested in Shakespeare," you say. "And anyway, he's too hard for them to read." Rubbish! They're not interested in teenage love? Jealousy? Murder and may-hem? Their lives aren't full of drama? Are you crazy? They *live* Shakespeare. If you can't connect kids with Shakespeare, you don't know what you're doing and you'd better get out of the field. Across America, teenagers say that literature courses are their worst courses. It's your fault. It's not Shakespeare's fault, or Keats's or Shelley's or Homer's. It's your fault.

You've got a serious problem here: You're supposed to be get-ting these kids ready for the real world and you haven't spent any time in the real world. You've been in schools all your life. You're supposed to help them understand themselves, but you don't appear to remember much about your life as a kid and you don't have any children yourself. You're supposed to empower them but you're something of a slave yourself and you're afraid to give them any more power than they already have. You're supposed to make them read and write, but you seldom read or write yourself. You're supposed to show them how handy mathematics can be, but you can't even balance your own checkbook. You're supposed to make them respect you, but you don't respect them. You're supposed to make them lifelong learners, but you were never very excited about learning in the first place and, in any case, you stopped learning anything significant years ago. Do you see the problem here?

4

Principals, it's your fault!

Aren't you the "building leader"? Then how come you're never in the building? Aren't you the "instructional leader"? Then how come you don't teach anything? What's with all the polyester clothes, all the beige tones and browns? Are you color blind too? I'm talking to you, coach.

You know, it might help if you learned something about management besides how to boss little kids around the gym. Being a teacher is not the best training for being a manager, either. It would help if you had some experience of management and leadership in the real world—you know, in companies that might go out of business if you don't do a good job. Your school will be in business no matter what you do. Screw up, and they'll just transfer you to another school where you can screw up again. And on and on. What's that you say? You have a "credential" in educational administration? Well, EXCUSE ME! They sure know a lot about management in higher ed, don't they? I'll bet your courses were barn-burners. Not.

Look, I want to help you out, here. I know that the district doesn't let you hire or fire anyone and I know that they don't give you any of your school's money to make financial decisions about and I know the union representative has more influence on your teachers than you do, but there are still a few things you can do to earn that salary you sold your teaching soul to get. Number one is GROW A BACKBONE. Stop asking permission for every little thing you or your teachers want to do. Just do it. The odds are heavy that the central office and the state and federal governments will never find out. If and when they do, it will be too late to take any significant action against you except, perhaps, to put a chastising memo into your file. And if what you and your teachers did was a good thing to do, and you had a backbone, you probably could delay any such memo forever with appropriate innuendoes about "legal action." Or you could ask for forgiveness, as the saying goes, instead of permission.

Number two, make some interesting decisions. I met a principal in Delaware who told his teachers to say five complimentary things each class period and five complimentary things during passing periods, for a total of about 40 per day for 5 straight days. He had 50 teachers, so that added up to 2000 compliments per day, 10,000 for the week. It changed the culture of the school. I met another principal who called himself the school's "chief learner." Day in and day out, he just modeled learning—asking questions, probing for evidence, thinking out loud, looking at issues from many points of view, and so forth. He asked his teachers to do the same. When Debbie Meier was principal of Central Park East, she insisted that everyone ask questions like "So what?" and, "Where are you coming from?" and, "What if?" One day, she was walking down the hall and overheard a girl telling her friend that a certain boy liked her. "What's the evidence for that?" snapped the friend. You can make things like that happen without the district's or the union's permission.

Number three, mess with kids' minds. They've got you pegged; they think they know everything you're going to do and say, because principals are as predictable as the sunrise. Throw them curveballs. Keep them off balance. For example, an angry teacher drags an angrier student into your office demanding he be punished for calling her something loathsome and disrupting class. Instead of giving him the usual song and dance (3-day sus-

pension, one step closer to being declared a "chronically disruptive student" and thus eligible for being expelled, etc.), try something like this:

"Why are you in school today?"
    "What do you mean? I *have* to be in school."
    "No you don't. You're 16. You can quit."
    "I'm 15."
    "I'm sure we could change the records. You're big for your
age. Leave it to me."
    "I can't quit."
    "Why not?"
    "My mother would kill me."
    "I'll talk to your mother. I think it's time you be out on your
own now, don't you? We're cramping your style, here, don't
you think? Making you follow all these rules and things.
Really, wouldn't it be nice to be out on your own?"
    "Are you telling me to quit school?"
    "I'm telling you to follow your heart, and it's obvious your
heart isn't in school."
    "You can't do that!"
    "I can't? I'm the principal. I can do whatever I want. And
anyway, it's clear you'd rather not be here. I'm only thinking of
your best interests."
    "But that's illegal!"
    "You get your lawyers, I'll get mine. But let's not focus on
that. Let's just think about how good it will feel to be rid of all
these fools in your life—Miss Wilson, me, all these jerks around
here. You could become one of those guys who hangs out over
there by the construction site, smoking and chatting with the
drunks. Wouldn't that be more fun?"

Curve balls like this work. The truth of the matter is, they're
just kids, and they're not as smart as they think. They're very easy
to manipulate. You just have to break type.
    Number four: Mess with teachers' minds. Teachers' minds are
the most important resource you have in the building. It is impor-

tant, first of all, that those minds be TURNED ON. Otherwise, teachers will just move about the building doing robotically what they observed teachers doing from the moment they went to kindergarten. The switch is located just below the brain, in the back. You can't see it, but you can tell whether it is off or on by the look in their eyes. To switch it on, say something totally unexpected, like, "What have you learned today?" You will hear a whirring noise as the teacher tries to process this unusual question. She may reply, "Do you mean what did I *teach* today?" indicating that the switch is still turned off. If you persist with something like, "No, what have you *learned* today, about teaching, learning, or particular students, that you didn't know when you arrived this morning?" you will hear more whirring and see a slight dilation of her pupils. The teacher's mind is now turned on. You will notice an acceleration of your pulse and hear a low whirring in your own brain, indicating that your mind is now moving into a somewhat higher gear, especially if the teacher has an answer, such as, "I noticed that I was trying so hard to stick to my lesson plan that I was missing little signals that some kids weren't listening to me." You may feel something expanding in your chest and will be prompted to say something like, "Tell me more about it. It sounds like a wonderful discovery." At this point, you may notice a flush in her cheek, a further indicator that her mind is not only turned on, but warming up. You, yourself, may experience a gentle thawing in a part of your brain's left hemisphere, a trickly sort of feeling, like a bead of sweat rolling down your forehead, only it's inside of your skull, not outside. This is a sure sign that you are experiencing a professional conversation.

Finally: Stop believing all that malarkey about how bad your school is and just draw conclusions from what you see right in front of your eyes. The truth is clear: These kids need far more than facts, spelling, and phonics; they need raising. These teachers can't take any more abuse. These parents, when they show up at all, are pains in the ass. These central office people have lost touch with reality. This superintendent doesn't have a clue. These school board members will throw you to the wolves if they get half a chance. Act accordingly.

5

Education schools, it's your fault!

Talk about wool gathering! The only reason your colleagues in other departments tolerate your presence in their academy is that you bring money into the university. And how do you bring money into the university? By arranging to have the State Department of Education create requirements for teacher and administrator certification that force people to take your rummy-dummy courses. Believe me, if they weren't forced to be there by law and economic necessity, they wouldn't be there at all. Do you really think anyone is taking your dreary library science course because they love the Dewey decimal system?

What a setup. Average students, compliant and unfocused; a subject no one has ever been able to pin down; a curriculum pretty much mirroring state certification laws; faculty who couldn't make it in a real discipline; and tenure, glorious tenure. A recipe for mediocrity if I ever saw one. To top it all off, *lectures*, hundreds and hundreds of lectures about how to teach, including lectures about how teachers probably shouldn't lecture in the classroom. Walk the halls and peer in the classrooms. What do you see? Lecturers blustering and slavish students taking notes, hour after hour, day after day. The sage on a stage. Few, if any, questions; little, if any, debate; no passion. Book learning. And what are the professors doing when they aren't lecturing? Writing papers that they can nervously read out-loud when they're on a six-person panel at the American Educational Research Association meeting in Indianapolis, the highlight of the year. Please.

Meanwhile, don't expect to see many professors out there in real schools trying to help real teachers. They're too busy doing "scholarship" about matters as irrelevant as they are arcane. Scholars have to find niches, of course, and the more scholars over the more years, the narrower the niches. Typical papers: "Gender Preference in Recitation Patterns During a Lesson on *Romeo and Juliet*," "Racial Stereotyping in Teen Pregnancy Counseling," "Male Privilege in Library Cataloguing," "The Present-Perfect

Tense in Ebonics," "Assessment of Basketball Skills Among Nine Students with Mild-to-Moderate Behavioral Disorders," "Social Class Interactions Among Special Students on a Botany Field Trip," "Ethnicity and the Pythagorean Theorem," "Information Processing in Three Diverse Classrooms," "Gender and Power in a Middle School Lunchroom," "Transdisciplinary Play-Based Assessment for the Low Incidence Disabled," "Reliability and Generalizability of the Grades A, B, and F in a Fifth-Grade Science Test over Time." Who publishes stuff like this? Why? Who reads it? No matter; it's all about getting tenure, and tenure is the name of the game.

Can't you see how pathetic this is? Your sense of inferiority is so *palpable*. You can blame some of it on your contemptuous colleagues who have real subject matter to work with, like chemistry, but most of this dreariness comes from your image of yourself, deep inside. *How you long to sound important!* Meanwhile, you're missing the boat! You're teaching your students all about gender and race and equity and ethnicity and multiculturalism and power, you're teaching them about stuff they can get anywhere else in the university—but you're not teaching them anything that will be remotely useful to them when they get into schools. Moreover, what you *are* teaching them, you're teaching in *bad ways*. Do you see the problem?

6

School board members, it's your fault!

Will you stop with the micromanaging already? You're supposed to be making the maps, not driving the car. You're like the Keystone cops: everybody driving, the car careening all over the road, guys falling off, guys jumping on, a cow on the bumper. You call this "governance"?

You're bulls in a china shop. I'm talking to you, Mr. Babbitt, who thinks schools should be run like businesses, and Miss Christian, who thinks schools should be churches, and you, Mr.

Demagogue, pretending you "represent" someone (how can you represent anyone when only 4% of the electorate votes in school board elections?), and you Mr. I Really Want to Be Mayor But This Was the Only Public Office Available. What a bunch of misfits! There should be some requirement that people like you should prove that they can get or keep *real* jobs before they're allowed to be on boards that tell people in real jobs what to do. And how about this, too: a requirement that you post your high school report cards when you announce your candidacies? It would help us to understand you.

Look, if you're really representing us, the general public, stop sitting on that dais like some satrap and come on down and sit with us in the hard chairs. Stop mooning at the television camera. Stop posturing for reporters and spend some time listening to real parents and real kids. Face reality: You're screwing the system up, even when you're good people, simply because you come and go like funny uncles, and each of you brings an agenda to inflict on unsuspecting teachers and administrators, and you're so *political*. How can a body of constantly changing strangers with single-interest-group agendas and an adversarial process contribute anything *but* instability and ferment to education? You're always changing things, you're always pulling the carrot out of the soil in order to see how it's growing, you're always reducing the beautiful complexity of learning to irrelevant test scores, which are never, of course, high enough. You're too far away from the action to really know what is going on, yet you won't let the people closest to the problems fix them.

Remind me again: What do we need you for? Democracy? Democracy would be letting people in the schools take care of their own problems. Accountability? Accountability would be letting the people in the schools take responsibility for their actions. Local control? Local control would be letting the people in the schools govern themselves. Managing the public trust? You call this management? You call this trust?

I know, I know—you're spending public money, most of which comes from people who don't have kids in school—who don't even *like* kids. They need to know that their property taxes are not being poured down a drain somewhere, right? And an elected school board gives them what—confidence? Assurance? I don't think so. A public utility commission could do the job just as well, and without all the hysterics and turnover.

Listen, I'm not sure we need you anymore. But if you're going to hang around, at least GET OUT OF THE WAY. Make it easier for teachers to teach, not harder. Make it easier for innovators to innovate, thinkers to think, passionate people to be passionate, excited learners to be excited about their learning, creative people to be creative, resourceful people to be resourceful, leaders to lead. Your job is to *liberate* energies, not smother them; *stir* imaginations, not extinguish them; *challenge* people, not thwart them, scold them, scare them, punish them, and drive them out of the field, weeping. Ask yourself why good people are leaving education or why other good people don't even think about entering it. What is there about the working environment and conditions that explains this? What can you do to improve that environment and change those conditions so that good people come into our schools and stay? Why don't you chew on that question for a while, instead of whether kids should know about condoms? Do you catch my drift?

7

Policy makers, it's your fault!

Has it ever occurred to you guys to *eliminate* some laws? All you do is just add more and more to an education code that's already the size of the Encyclopedia Britannica. No one knows what's in there anymore, least of all you. You could cross out every other education law and no one would know the difference. Have you read any of that stuff lately? It's either absurdly broad ("the state will have a thorough and efficient education system") or myopically specific ("a United States flag will be displayed in every classroom at all times"). You've made education the most overregulated undertaking in America, and you wonder why it's not efficient. *It's not efficient because it takes a bureaucracy and a half to sort through all your bizarre laws and figure out what to do with them.* Back off, will you?

I'm talking to you, Representative Neanderthal. It's the twenty-first century and you're sponsoring another bill to restrict the teaching of evolution. Do you have any idea how stupid you look to the rest of the civilized world? Can you imagine how gullible you look for buying into this phony baloney notion of "creation science"? A fine example you're setting for children. I've got a tip for you: People who propose education legislation should at least appear educated. You say you're only representing your constituents? Keep this in mind: Most people didn't vote in the election and of those who did, you barely eked out a plurality, and of them, only a handful are as moronic as you are. You don't have a constituency. You're a legislator because most people don't care who's in the job. If you don't have any intelligence to display, at least show some humility. And bone up on the Constitution and American history in your spare time, will you? Your bill to post the Ten Commandments in every classroom won't pass judicial muster this year, next year, or ever. If you want a religious state, join the Taliban.

I see you sniggering, Senator Marx. That bill you sponsored on providing AIDS instruction to elementary school students belongs in the same toilet as Representative Neanderthal's bill. These are *children,* man! Have you no shame? And all your "sensitivity" bills and multiculturalism mandates and revisionist history standards and on and on. Don't you see that you and Neanderthal are twins? He wants government to use the schools for religious proselytizing, and you want government to use the schools for political proselytizing. He wants government to get rid of Halloween parties in school, and you want government to get rid of Christmas trees in school. He wants to ban *Catcher in the Rye* and you want to ban *Huckleberry Finn.* You're peas in a pod.

We're over here trying to teach kids to be thoughtful, to think critically and weigh evidence before jumping to conclusions, to evaluate their conduct and change it when necessary, to be tolerant of diverse views, and to be civil to one another. You're not making our job any easier. How can I tell a 14-year-old not to overreact, when that seems to be all you do, besides nothing? How can I tell a 15-year-old to abjure simplistic overgeneralizations, when that is your stock in trade? We bring the newspaper into the classroom to study current events, and when kids see your shenanigans, they just roll their eyes. "Who are these guys?" they ask. "Your representatives," we answer. "Why are they so stupid?" they ask. "They're not stupid," we say. "They just sound that way." "Why do they sound that way?" they persist. "Because that's how politics works," we rationalize. "Why is politics so stupid?" On and on. Statements I wouldn't let an eighth grader get away with show up unchallenged every day in the newspaper and on the television news, parroted by "newsreaders."

Do I have to be more specific? Do I have to list the pieces of totally foolish legislation that pour out of our legislatures day in and day out? The incomprehensible campaign rhetoric, the vitriolic political attacks, the mind-numbingly stupid policy initiatives that persist despite overwhelming evidence that they're ineffective at best, counterproductive, at worst? The xenophobia, the paranoia, the hip shooting, the carelessness, the racism, the demagoguery, the hypocrisy, the bald-faced lying, the slander, the muck throwing, the vilifying? The stupefying obscurantism, the monotony, the pretentiousness, the utter dearth of substance in almost everything you say? Is this why I'm busting my pick here trying to teach them to read and write and think: so they can sound like *you*?

Give me something to work with, here—a well-written sentence, a witty quip, an intelligent allusion to history or literature, a stimulating metaphor, a speech worth reading and talking about. Show me some class—an interest in ideas and genuine debate, a fondness for language, a generous imagination, a sign, however faint, that you're capable of learning and changing. That's how you can help me the most. Not by proposing more legislation about "holding schools accountable," but by publicly respecting the English language, by publicly demonstrating the value of critical thinking, by publicly observing the virtues of civility, by crafting your words and policies as if you were teaching children— which, of course, you are.

8

Let's face it: It's OUR fault!

We can't agree about much. We fight all the time. If you talk to people about the purposes of schooling, they're all over the map. The founding fathers thought that a school system was necessary for cultivating virtue and developing a "natural" aristocracy based on merit instead of wealth, birth, or accidents of history. Most people today seem to believe that the chief purpose of schools is to pass on "academic" knowledge and skills, although the word *academic*, when applied to a person or an idea, usually is used pejoratively, and although they don't agree about *which* knowledge and *which* skills, as I will shortly demonstrate. Others will tell you that the chief purpose of schools is to develop workers (an idea the founding fathers explicitly rejected). If you point out that what students learn in school has almost nothing to do with the world of work, they'll say that the *habits* picked up in school—industry, obedience, punctuality, and competitiveness, for instance—are what really matter. Still other people will tell you that the primary purpose of schooling is socialization: Every child has to learn how to get along with the group, how to be a good neighbor, how to exercise the kind of civic responsibility likely to keep a democracy alive.

Another large group of people will tell you that the primary purpose of schooling is to develop the little genius that hides inside each of us, to unleash our creativity and help us find and exercise our sacred voices. Some will tell you that it is about baby-sitting or keeping the young out of the workforce or that it's a giant credentialing machine designed simply to sort people. Many policy makers appear to believe that the primary purpose of the school system is to correct the social and economic inequities generated by the larger society. To them and their followers, it is all about "leveling the playing field" and fighting injustice. Pockets of parents will tell you that schooling is about itself, like learning is about itself or growing up is about itself; such things don't need ulterior justifications or extrinsic purposes. There's some truth in all of these beliefs.

But here's the problem: No system can serve all of these purposes equally well, and if you put priority on one of them, you get a very different curriculum and organization than you would get if you put priority on another. A system devoted primarily to college preparation is different from a system devoted primarily to workforce preparation or socialization or social justice. A system designed to support democracy is different from a system designed to support economic expansion. The view of a parent is different from the view of a student, a teacher, a principal, a professor of education, a school board member, a bureaucrat, or a policy maker. They don't see the same thing and don't have the same roles to play in the system.

It gets worse. If you go back to the academic purposes of schooling and ask people what subjects are most important, you get the Tower of Babel. Large groups of people disagree strongly about what subjects should be in the curriculum and, within subjects, what facts and skills should be taught or ignored. The founding fathers disagreed among themselves, today's general public disagrees with the experts, people with postsecondary education disagree with people who never went beyond high school, older Americans disagree with younger Americans, the rich disagree with the poor (the report to read is *What Americans Believe Students Should Know: A Survey of U.S. Adults,* by Marzano, Kendall, and Cicchinelli, 1998). Of 248 standards in 15 subject areas, only 102 are strongly endorsed by more than half of Americans and only 33 garner support from two-thirds of us, according to a Gallup Poll conducted for this study. These differences in values are fundamental and will not go away. What we have here is a constantly shifting current of public and political opinion, with no hope of consensus about anything except the most basic commitment to reading, writing, and arithmetic—a woefully low set of expectations. In such circumstances, is it any wonder that the system seems incoherent and faddish or that someone, somewhere, is always angry at the schools about something they're not doing?

Yet, what do we do with the fact that most Americans give their children's schools—the schools they have been in, the schools they know—passing grades? Is it possible that the judgment of common people is as valid as any "expert's" or politician's? Is it possible that most schools actually are doing a pretty good job and that the system is better than we think it is when we are analyzing it intellectually? What are we to make of the fact that, day after day, millions of adults and tens of millions of children come home from their jobs in schools with joy and with satisfaction in their day's work? Where in our school reform calculus do we factor in the millions upon millions of friendships and intimacies and confidences, the sheer mega-tonnage of love in its various forms, which pervade the classrooms, halls, and playgrounds? How do we take account of the fact that at graduation ceremonies, grown men weep like babies, angry teenagers embrace their teachers, and, for a time, no one blames anyone for anything?

Is it possible that what we are all to blame for is shortsightedness and lack of perspective? Is it possible that, given such a contentious and diverse population and such preposterous ideals and such a maddeningly contradictory political and economic system and such a history of ambivalence about the young and such a history of penny pinching when it comes to investing in the young, America has about as good an education system as could reasonably be expected? Is it possible that, in the circumstances, we are all getting pretty much what we want and what we deserve?

There. I feel better now.

CHAPTER 5

On Leading, Misleading, and Unleading

1

I never thought much about leadership until I was a junior in high school. One day, I was out sick and my best friend Jim called me up after school to tell me that both of us had been nominated for president and vice president of the student government. "Let's run together," he said. "I'll run for president and you be my vice president."

Anyone would have predicted this. Since third grade, he had been a leader and I had been his sidekick. But for some reason, and without even thinking about it, I said, "Why don't *I* run for president and you be *my* vice president?" We were both stunned. Such a possibility had never occurred to either one of us before. He repeated his first proposal and I repeated mine. "But I don't want to be a vice president," he said. "Me neither," I said. So we decided to run against each other.

I won by eight votes, because of a head cold that deepened my voice during a decisive campaign speech. My campaign manager said I got the Gregory Peck vote. I don't remember much about my leadership except that I wrote a monthly column in the school newspaper exhorting teenagers to prove to the world that they were not as bad as everyone thinks.

Whatever leadership qualities I might have had then, they went underground for a good long while during college and graduate school and my years working on educational assessments. My interest in leadership began to surface again only when I found myself at the Education Commission of the States working with, and writing for, politicians and corporate CEOs. It happened that most of them were persuaded that the single greatest obstacle to school improvement was lack of leadership of the right kind. Whatever the education problem, we could trace its roots to failures of leadership and find a solution in some new kind of leadership. Throughout the 1970s and 1980s, institutes of leadership, leadership gurus, and conferences on leadership flourished. Books on leadership appeared like blossoms in spring. Our conversations were about collaborative leadership, transformational leadership, visionary leadership, leadership for change, servant leadership, participative leadership, authoritarian leadership, authoritative leadership, leadership for results, principle-centered leadership, value-based leadership, facilitative leadership, artful leadership, the Tao of leadership, entrepreneurial leadership, situational leadership, inner-path leadership, and charismatic leadership, to name the ones that come first to mind. Each had its day in the sun, each was embraced by one reform-oriented leader or another. I read about them all and incorporated them into political speeches and articles about school reform.

My own leadership style was traditional. As a senior manager in a medium-sized nonprofit organization, I sat on a management team that made all the major decisions and passed them on to the employees. My opportunity to practice some of these new approaches to leadership arose when I left that job to start P.S. 1 Charter School, and even then I was not immediately conscious that I was practicing a particular style. To begin with, I had no followers to lead. I called friends over to the house and we sat around and talked about what would be ideal. Then, fast-moving events began to dictate what had to be done and the order in which things had to be done. I could plan at a very general level, but medium- and fine-grained plans were useless because they were rendered obsolete so quickly. People began calling and showing up, so I worked with whoever was present. Strangely, the right people kept showing up at the right time. Just when I needed a certain kind of expertise and had begun despairing of ever finding it, the phone would ring and it was someone with that expertise. Along the way, some graduate students joined our meetings and began studying our design process. One of them wrote a paper about me and concluded that I was a charismatic, visionary leader. I didn't feel very charismatic (few people shared my belief that we could get a charter school off the ground in Denver), and whatever vision I had seemed to shift every time someone new came into the circle. Apparently, though, I had a leadership style.

I think that whatever leadership I began to practice derived less from my readings about leadership and more from the ideas at the heart of the school we were designing and from the flow of events. For instance, "community" was a key aspect of what we wanted to create. We were starting the school as part of the development of a square block of old buildings downtown, owned by The Tattered Cover Bookstore, a very friendly, community-oriented enterprise. Besides a new bookstore, the project was to include small retail "mom and pop" shops that would hearken back to turn-of-the-twentieth-century neighborhoods in which people knew each other and felt part of a community. Multipriced apartments would bring together people from different socioeconomic strata. Our school would bring together people of all ages, day and night, for communal learning. The project would create, we said, an "urban village."

In my own studies of successful schools, I had concluded that the most efficient and effective ones create and sustain a sense of community. I had come to agree with Glenn Tinder (1980) that "community is inquiry." In his thoughtful book, *Community: Reflections on a Tragic Ideal*, Tinder writes:

> The familiar idea that community consists in agreement of any
> kind, that it consists, for example, in common acceptance of a nar-
> row and stifling set of customs inherited from the past, or in wide-
> spread acceptance of an advertising message, grossly distorts
> human nature and obscures the ideal of community. It tends to rec-
> oncile human beings to social conditions under which they are far
> less than they should be and are estranged from one another even
> though they may be totally united through whatever forms of trun-
> cated selfhood they have accepted. . . . Only cooperation in the most
> serious human concerns—and this means above all in the explo-

ration of being—calls forth a community. . . . *Community, presumably, lies in sharing the truth, and if this is so it must be inherent in the very process of searching for the truth.* (p. 31, emphasis added)

Great classrooms, I had learned, are places where people are searching for, and trying to understand, the truth; great schools are places where people are searching for, and trying to understand, the truth. Great communities are places where people are searching for, and trying to understand, the truth. The truth lies as much in the search itself as in any result of the search. Community is an active process, inseparable from the questions that animate it. It is a kind of discourse. Want to start a community? Start asking tough questions.

We agreed early on that our charter school would be organized around the asking of tough questions because that is how a sense of community is engendered. And, since it was located in the heart of downtown, the school would specialize in asking tough questions about cities and city life. Parents, teachers, and students would be engaged in exploring the nature of being-in-community, especially in the context of diverse, urban environments. The key to success would be a kind of leadership that created and sustained a kind of discourse that led consistently to learning, rather than to fragmentation, polarization, ethnic or class gridlock, or the erosion of belief in a common good.

Our ideas about learning itself also influenced the kinds of leadership we prized. For us, learning is a social, not just an individual, activity. Individuals learn with and through others, and knowledge is a group possession. The school would have to be set up to facilitate social learning, to enable people from all walks of life to share their expertise and tap into group knowledge. We summed up what we wanted to emphasize about learning in seven statements.

1. learning begins with what the learner is interested in;
2. learning is an active, constructive, meaning-making process, not a passive experience;
3. learning is a consequence of thinking;
4. the best learning is coherent, connected, memorable, and useful, like a story;

5. learning requires truthfulness, humility, courage, respectfulness, tolerance, civility, and faith;
6. learning requires diverse perspectives around the table;
7. anyone can learn whatever he or she is motivated to learn, given appropriate opportunities to learn.

These ideas suggest that learning is a *transformative experience*—that is, it literally transforms the learner's body of knowledge, ways of thinking, and ways of acting in the world. If these were going to be the thoughts around which the instructional program and, indeed, the school culture would be built, they also had to be the touchstones of our design process itself. If we could not honor those key ideas before the school was established, we doubted we would be able to honor them once it was up and running. But to honor them meant to embrace a certain kind of leadership, if we were going to practice what we were preaching. It would have to be a leadership that sought out and built upon people's interests; that helped people construct or find meaning in what they were doing; that was thoughtful; that helped people learn and tell stories; that honored truthfulness, humility, courage, respectfulness, tolerance, civility, and faith; that provided the necessary requirements for learning; and that assumed that everyone was capable of learning.

Another influence on the kind of leadership I came to practice was the flow of events. Opportunities and problems cropped up randomly and in bunches. I could not plan for most of them and I could not deal with them in a linear, rational, systematic way. We were often ignorant of the major variables we needed to control and could not control them even when we found out what they were. Many of our tasks were contradictory. For example, we couldn't get a charter unless we had a facility, but we couldn't negotiate a facility lease without a charter. We couldn't get a charter without an instructional staff, but we couldn't make financial commitments to potential staff without the charter. We needed families to get the charter, but families were skeptical that we would ever be granted a charter and had to make decisions about where to place their children before we would find out if the board would fund us. We needed money to keep fighting and to cover projected startup expenses, but potential funders needed to see a charter before they could commit. The board had said it would not grant a charter unless we prespecified our curriculum in minute detail; our position was that since we were providing personal learning plans for each student, the details would have to be specified by the parents, students, and staff once the school was opened. The board wanted us to conform to the district's curriculum goals, objectives, and tests; we argued that our job as a charter school was to be innovative and to offer a clear choice to parents. There was no logical way through such conundrums. When you don't know the variables and can't control the ones you do know and find yourself faced with multiple, interrelated conundrums—when you are *in complexity*—you have to resort to other modes of action. You have to learn what to do when you reach a point at which you don't know what to do. The most useful models came to me not from the literature of leadership, but from the arts. What does the painter do when the painting doesn't "work"? What does the poet do when the poem isn't "right"? How does the storyteller tell the story when he doesn't know how it will end? The key to leadership in complex situations that do not yield to rational planning is to become a better and better juggler, keeping as many balls in the air as you can, plus three more. You are keeping *possibility itself* alive, knowing that sooner or later some opportunities or problems will eliminate themselves, some will be eliminated by unforeseen factors or bad timing, and some will transform themselves into other problems and opportunities that you know how to solve or take advantage of. This takes great patience and an unshakable belief that the problems *will* either go away or get solved, new opportunities *will* arise, and you *will* triumph, ultimately.

The flow of events and the ways in which people came to enlist in our cause led to our first major "rule" about leadership: *If you think that you are the right person, in the right place, at the right time, with the right expertise and the right passion and the right network to get something done, then take the lead!* When there are a thousand head of cattle milling around in Texas and you've got to get the cattle drive going and someone says, "Montana's thisaway," you follow the guy who seems to know where he's going—especially if you've never been to Montana. All anyone had to do was persuade us that he or she was the right person in those ways—the right person to design our approach to computers or the right person to design our approach to literacy—and we'd follow his or her lead.

A corollary to that rule was, *if you're the one who identified the problem, you take the lead in getting it solved.* We noticed that at most of the neighborhood meetings we attended, someone would stand up and ask some leader to solve a problem that he or she didn't even know existed. For instance, someone would say, "There's a whole bunch of broken glass out in the alley behind my store and X [an authority of some kind] hasn't picked it up." My thought was always, "Why don't you pick it up yourself?" The dark side of representative government is that people are always ragging on their leaders and their bureaucracies to solve problems they could just as easily and more quickly solve themselves. It's as if all sense of personal responsibility for getting anything done is abandoned as soon as there is some elected representative to complain to.

I didn't want to be the kind of leader who goes around solving problems that the problem finders could just as easily solve, because it seemed to me that when people are compelled to solve a problem that they didn't even know was a problem in the first place, they don't tend to do a very good job. Moreover, I had seen too many communities in which people were sitting around bellyaching and waiting for some outsider to come in and fix their neighborhoods. I had seen too many students sitting around waiting for some teacher or principal or parent to solve their problems. If our goal was to build a sense of community, we needed a kind of leadership that builds responsibility. It seemed to me that *a leader takes responsibility for other people taking responsibility*, and that's a very different thing from the notion of the leader *who takes responsibility for everything.* If you're going to be the second kind of leader, you spend an enormous amount of time trying to solve problems that someone else has identified, that don't particularly interest you, and that you may well be incompetent to solve. If you're going to be the first kind of leader, you spend much of your time creating situations that encourage people to take responsibility for solving their problems and improving their lives.

2

I'm using the word *leader* to apply to people who lead others to do things they might not have done without the leader's influence. How do they do this? What is the source of their power to influence others? Some say it is charisma—a gift vouchsafed by the gods, a special grace. Over the centuries, charismatic leaders have been thought to be divinely inspired prophets, healers, and messengers. Having been labeled a charismatic leader, I find this is a little unsettling. Even in its more pedestrian use—denoting a person of great charm—the word *charismatic* cannot get away from suggestions of something magic or supernatural. The assertion remains that charisma is some kind of mysterious power that can *charm* us, *overpower* us, *transport* us, *influence* us—that is, *flow into* us from outside us—and *affect* us, independently of our will. We are standing there, minding our own business, and someone with charisma comes up and casts some kind of spell over us. Charisma appears to bypass our capacities to reason objectively and go right for our emotions. The charismatic leader is apparently some kind of wizard. We follow him not because we have weighed his words and persuaded ourselves that we should follow, but because we cannot help following, regardless of reason. Or perhaps reasoning powers are irrelevant to the experience. Perhaps, through the charismatic, we are tuned into some greater power, some higher truth than mere reason could attain even if we engaged it.

Bill Clinton is the most charismatic person I have ever met. He could walk unannounced into Times Square on New Year's Eve and within moments everyone would feel his presence. It's like he emits pheromones (which eventually may prove to be a better explanation of charisma than the divine one). He illustrates the central problem with charismatic leadership: that people are mysteriously attracted to him and eventually feel that he somehow wooed them, took them off their guard, romanced them—misled them. It does not occur to people who are attracted to charismatic figures that they had some choice in the matter, some responsibility for electing to follow or love or believe such a person. Rather, they feel as if they were bewitched, hypnotized, or hornswoggled.

Others are repelled by charismatic figures. If someone is charming, watch out! You can't trust someone who is disarming, who instantly bypasses your rational defenses, and somehow distracts you from paying close, critical attention to his words. You want to be persuaded by his arguments, not his life force, pheromones, divine inspiration, or sex appeal.

There is something of the erotic in charisma. The associations are ancient and persistent. At its best, eros is simply love, writ large—the connecting power of the universe, the force that draws bee to flower, lover to lover, eye to beauty. I've often thought that learning is a species of love, and it's not unusual for students to fall in love, in a certain kind of way, with their teachers and their teachers' ideas. Didn't Whitehead say the first stage of learning is the romantic stage? Perhaps we fall in and out of love with our leaders, too. Freud probably would say so. Our first leaders are our parents. It is from them that we learn about love and it is upon their love that so much of our adult productivity and happiness depends. Authority figures, like leaders, may elicit this earliest, prototypical love, or we instinctively may offer it, whether they want it or not. The transference of our childish love to someone else is fraught with dangers if it comes complete with unresolved fear and rage and complex, unrequited, or dysfunctional emotions. Watch out, authority figure! The analyst or therapist is trained to deal with these transferences, but the average boss or leader is not. On his or her shoulders rest, then, not only all those associations with gods, magic, and the supernatural, but, in addition, the even more volatile transferences of people for whom Dad and Mom were awesome beings, capable of either protecting them from danger or eating them alive.

The more you think about it, the less appealing it is to be a leader, especially a charismatic one. You can't possibly live up to your followers' beliefs in your supernatural powers or their transferences of unconscious feelings. Sooner or later, you are bound to let them down, the way gods, moms, and dads tend to do. Sooner or later some of your followers must rebel against you, as they tend to do against their gods, moms, and dads. You will be found out to be human, not supernatural. You will be shown to be no better than the rest of us—in fact, worse, much worse, because you presumed to be so divine, so stuck up. You will be discovered to love another, as Mom loved Dad and Dad loved Mom, and that will make someone *very* angry at you. Sooner or later, you will be discovered to be a phony and a seducer, as Dad was a phony when he said you were his little girl, and his alone. Sooner or later, you will be expected to throw a follower out into the world as the poor, unready follower was thrown into a cruel world by his parents, or abandoned by them when they had the nerve to die or take an interest in their own lives. In anticipation of being thrown out, a follower will want to throw you out first. In anticipation of your phoniness, a follower will want to unearth your secrets and scrutinize your every word for the lies he knows are there. The mob delights in exposing all leaders, sooner or later, as hypocrites.

Thus it is that the other side of the leading coin is misleading. Leaders are expected, at some level and by some followers, to mislead, especially if they are charismatic. The very fact that they don the mantle of leadership suggests a certain pride—and pride goeth, as we know, before a fall. Your intentions have nothing to do with this; your honesty and integrity have nothing to do with this. If you presume to be a leader, you inevitably will mislead *somebody*; and if you do not mislead somebody, you most certainly will mislead yourself.

As long as we think our leaders possess some power that has been denied us ordinary mortals; as long as their charisma is a force that relieves us of any responsibility for choosing to follow them; as long as we are passive or subconscious participants in the transactions of leadership and followership, unaccountable for our passivity and our transferences, both we and our leaders will share a deeply ambivalent relationship and reap its consequences.

3

One day a woman came up to me after a meeting and said, "Give me some power."

"What kind of power do you want?" I asked.

"Some of your power," she said.

"I don't have any power to give you," I said. "You'll have to find your own power."

She went away discouraged and I went away wondering what this power thing was all about. Is that what's at the heart of leadership—power? Was I leading this effort because I wanted or needed power? Was I hogging all the power? Power to do what? I certainly believed in "empowerment," but I hadn't really looked at the concept closely. What is the source of leadership's power and how is it given to, or taken from, others?

Power is simply the ability to act or to do things. Associated with it, however, are notions of vigor, energy, strength, authority, and influence. Here we are again, dealing with something that, like charisma, suggests a fundamental animating force that some people have, or acquire, and others do not. Some people feel a greater sense of power to act and do things than others. Some people literally *have* more power to act in certain venues, by dint of their social position, trappings, or associations with other powerful people. It appears that some babies are just born with a sense of power and efficacy. The world is there to be mastered. Other babies are born shy and fearful, tentative about their actions, uncertain about their place in the scheme of things. Moreover, many children, regardless of their original sense of powerfulness, learn through the vicissitudes of life to feel and act more or less powerfully.

Power seems to come in two forms: inner power and outer power. Inner power seems to be the power to find and marshal one's energies and talents and to carry them into action. We all have inner power of some kind and to some degree; anyone can tap into this to maximize his or her effectiveness. Outer power is shaped by social position, historical situation, economic circumstances, and impersonal constraints on freedom to act in various domains. Outer power can be power over other people's scope for exercising their inner power. Outer power can determine who is accepted and who is rejected, who works and who does not, who lives and who dies. Outer power can be human and temporal or it can be divine. Some have thought that divine power is the greatest power of all and the source of all other power. Some have thought that inner power is really a manifestation of divine power, which would be great if it were true, since we could ignore all the forms of outer earthly power that we don't like. And some have thought that the only power worth worrying about is earthly, temporal, social power to effect events in the here and now.

The woman who asked me to give her power was asking for a commodity of some kind. Had there been an organization at the time, this would have been like requesting a promotion, a job with more responsibility and scope for exercising power. However, we had no jobs to hand out. People needed to step up and say, "I'll do this thing that no one else is doing." The power she needed was the power to propose what to do and then do it. Even if I had a position for her—a position of power—she would have found that it was of little value without her inner power. People who lack a sense of their inner power often believe that a position of outer power will make them more powerful, but this is seldom true except in a trivial sense. You can occupy a position of power even if you have no sense of inner power, but you cannot exercise the power of the position effectively. People can tell immediately that you are hiding your impotence in the trappings of power and they react accordingly. There is no substitute for inner power.

Empowerment is not about giving someone power they don't have. It is about giving them opportunities to discover and exercise the power they do have. A leader who empowers others is not "delegating." He is identifying the constraints that others have placed upon their actions and helping them find ways to break free. His job is to enable each person to exercise the power most appropriate to his or her talents and interests. It is not to make everyone "equally" powerful, whatever that means, or to make everyone the leader. These turned out to be important distinctions for me, not widely understood.

During the 2 years it took to plan and organize P.S. 1, a number of contributors to the effort were heartfelt, if dogmatic, "democrats," and they urged us to use "democratic decision making" and act only on "consensus." They were wary of all kinds of power and very suspicious of leaders, preferring "facilitators," "coordinators," and other informal, rotating roles that ensured "full participation" and "equity." As critically important as these concepts and values are—and as quintessentially American as they are—they mask a deep-seated fear of authority. Most of the people I know who are true believers in purely democratic procedures—and there are many of them in the alternative schools movement and community organizing—are opposed to most other forms of authority in society and the family. Many are enamored of primitive tribes and non-Western cultures where there are supposedly no social hierarchies, power is widely shared, and "leaders," as we know them, do not exist. For them, either you are a democrat or you are a dictator. There is nothing in between. Either you believe in *all the people* making decisions or you believe in *the few* making decisions; and if you believe in the few, you are clearly on the side of the privileged, the rich, the elite, and the authoritarian, all of whom are morally corrupt. Anyone who presumes to be a leader presumes to be better than others and is therefore automatically unworthy of being followed. This, I imagine, is the reason why the crabs in the bottom of the kettle pull the one who's trying to show them the way out back into the boiling water.

Even if a leader puts aside the silliness of extreme political correctness, she must still balance democratic values, such as full and equal participation, against utilitarian values, such as *getting things done at the right time and in the right ways to ensure that the group meets the goal that everyone wants to achieve.* A great process with no result may satisfy some, but most people prefer a result first and will settle for a less than perfect process. Leaders have to remember that democracy is not an end in itself; it is a means to other ends, such as a sound organization or the Good Society. Get too bogged down in the process and you will not achieve your ends; ignore the process and you will get unexpected, wrongheaded, or transitory ends.

Once again, my cues about the appropriate form of leadership for developing P.S. 1 came from our understanding of the kind of learning we wanted to promote at the school—transformative, experiential learning. The question of how democratic our decision-making process should be was answerable by asking how democratic transformational teaching and experiential learning are. The answer is that they are far more democratic than other forms of teaching and learning, but they nevertheless require the exercise of important forms of authority and authoritativeness. They are not *purely* democratic. The questions of the learner are extremely important, of course; but they are meaningless without the teacher's counter questions, guiding dialogue, and capacity to *lead* (the root of the word educate is *educere*, to lead forth) the learner toward the experiences and sources of knowledge necessary to find satisfactory answers. To be sure, both can play teacher and learner in the transaction; but at any given moment, one is the teacher and one is the learner, one is more authoritative than the other, in the sense that one possesses more *due authority* by dint of greater lore, deeper insight, or stronger argument. Whether learners are children or adults, they need sooner or later to turn to the *authorities* on various subjects, the people who have thought about them before and have distinguished themselves by their persuasiveness or depth of knowledge. The authorities can be wrong, of course, but both personal and social knowledge advance by engaging the authorities and improving on them, not by ignoring them altogether. Yes, children know a lot and can learn a lot by themselves, but significant learning is a *conversation.* Autodidacts are poor teachers and worse learners.

The kind of leadership that made the most sense for us was leadership that was itself a form of transformative learning—not only because we were starting a school, but also because we were all learning how to do it as we went along. I heard of a principal once who called himself the school's "chief learner." That's the idea. However, if you're going to lead as a learner, you must understand that there are people who want their teachers and their leaders to *already know* everything. They don't *want* to learn, if learning means making mistakes, or going off in wrong directions, or adapting to information that didn't exist when you started out. The fact is, most of us do not like learning things that cause discomfort or require major and frequent changes of mind and habit. We want to learn what is easy or even fun for us to learn. So if you build your leadership around the necessity for everyone, including the leader, to learn, don't be surprised if some people resist the idea or don't get it. And if you go further to assert that learning requires certain kinds of submission to higher authorities, don't be surprised if you lose adherents who will not submit to anything or anyone, on the grounds that to do so would violate their democratic values.

A leader purports to be doing things for others; therefore, he must honor the wishes of those others and know their intentions and values intimately, if he is to do a good job of carrying out their wishes. But if a leader does nothing *but* carry out the exact wishes of others, he's not a leader. He's a follower. This paradox bedevils both weak leaders and weak followers. Weak leaders do not want to get out ahead of the followers, lest they be abandoned. They're always polling followers to find out what to do next. Weak followers do not really want to be led; they want to tell their leaders what to do every step of the way. Both are driven by multiple fears, including the fear of being, or being perceived to be, antidemocratic.

This bothered me a lot, at first. Charter schools represent a democratic impulse, an uprising of ordinary citizens against an authoritarian school district, with its powerful unions and school boards and bureaucrats. Charter school founders are in the tradition of homesteaders and entrepreneurs, "little people" who want to do things *their* way. A charter school should be designed and governed by parents, teachers, and students, and it should teach the democratic citizenship our nation relies on for its survival by being, itself, an exemplar of democratic citizenship. I was very sensitive to the thought—my own or someone else's—that I might lead this enterprise in an "undemocratic" way. Yet it needed leadership or it was never going to happen. I knew that I had the political, financial, and educational networks and the knowledge and skills necessary to launch something like this in a hostile environment, and I knew it was the right time in my life to tackle this kind of challenge. I saw no one else both capable of doing it and ready to do it. Everyone acknowledged that I was leading the effort. But I was reluctant to assert any authority beyond persuasiveness of argument. This was fine until we had grant money to be allocated and decisions to be made about who actually would work in the school. Group decision making becomes far more difficult when money and power enter the picture.

All leaders have to come to terms with power. Even if you believe you do not have any, someone else believes you do. Even if you believe power is widely shared, someone else believes you are keeping the lion's share. Even if you believe you are helping others discover and unleash their own inner power, someone else believes you are exercising yours, and doesn't like it. Perhaps because we were all children and spent the most vulnerable years of our lives subject to the arbitrary exercise of power by people who were much bigger than us; perhaps because we have had unpleasant experiences with teachers or police or agencies or institutions or a government; perhaps because we have experienced the impotence of poverty or discrimination; or perhaps just because we are Americans—we are all a little prickly about power, and some of us are much pricklier than others. We all want as much power as we can get and we all want limitations on the power of others.

If the advocates for pure democracy present one way of trying to constrain leaders' power, the advocates of "accountability" through bureaucratic processes present another very common way of constraining power. The word *accountability* has quantitative roots. To account is literally to count; to account for is literally to reckon for money held in trust. Eventually, the word came to mean, "give a satisfactory reason for," and accountability became, "liability to give account of and answer for, discharge of duties or conduct." Whereas pure democracy advocates fear any kind of authority, accountability advocates permit authority, but only on the condition that any authority reports to some other authority, which reports to some other authority, and so on. Every leader must report to a board of directors, a legislative body, or "the people" in some institutionalized form. Every leader who spends money is accountable to the people who give her money and to (of course) *accountants*— who are accountable to "generally accepted accounting principles." Every leader is expected to follow the existing laws.

Nevertheless, as everyone knows, great leaders often see that they must punch through all the conventional constraints that define the status quo in order to do something extraordinary. Gandhi and Martin Luther King frequently broke the law, because the law *itself* was a part of the problem they were trying to solve. Thomas Jefferson skirted around constitutional processes in order to acquire the Louisiana Territory. Many presidents have conducted important public business secretly. Many a successful entrepreneur has had to bet "on the come" and keep creditors at bay until the company strikes some kind of oil. Leaders tend to take risks. Boards, oversight committees, legislative bodies, and accountants tend not to take risks. Indeed, their role is usually to eliminate or minimize risks.

It is perfectly sensible for us to want our leaders to account for their conduct, one way or another. Any leader worth his or her salt should, in fact, consult with various people before making major decisions, including elders, mentors, and people likely to be affected by the decisions. But if you put too many constraints on leaders' capacities to exercise their judgment, you smother the leadership. Leaders require more latitude than the rest of us have, more freedom to act, more trust—at least until they screw up. They also require more latitude in their explanations of their conduct. If they must make note of every aspect of a decision and file detailed accounts of their every move, they will be so busy thinking about what they are doing they won't be able to do it. If they must communicate everything to every conceivable stakeholder, in the terms most understandable to that stakeholder and at a time most convenient for the stakeholder, they will likewise fail to lead. Fear of power—whether it takes the form of ultra democratic processes or ultra accountability practices—leads inevitably to impotence. All approaches to constraining power tend toward dysfunctionality when they fall into the hands of zealots. For the zealot, there can never be enough paperwork, enough documentation, enough communication, enough accounting, enough reporting, for the simple reason that he or she does not have enough trust.

The concept of accountability lacks logical limits. We have to count on common sense to tell us when we have gone too far. If the risk of too little accountability is dictatorship of various kinds, the risk of too much accountability is Max Weber's Iron Cage of bureaucratic rationality.

4

It is fashionable to want "visionary" leaders, but I have been called a visionary leader and even I am in considerable doubt about what that means. Once again, we're using a word with supernatural connotations. According to the dictionary, a vision is "something which is apparently seen otherwise than by ordinary sight; *esp.* an appearance of a prophetic or mystical character, or having the nature of a revelation, supernaturally presented to the mind either in sleep or in an abnormal state." The most I can say about my visionary powers is that at one time I imagined that a school might exist that did not, at that time, exist. Nothing about the imagined school was original. Many of the elements existed in schools or learning centers somewhere, and I had seen them with my ordinary sight. They just didn't exist all together in one particular place. Other elements could be imagined to arise naturally in conversations with ordinary people about the kinds of schools they wanted their children to attend. Nothing mystical or prophetic here.

Many organizations create "vision statements" and go through a "visioning process." This usually involves asking people what they want to see happen in 5 or 10 or more years, what they want the organization to look like. These visions can range from the overly vague—"I want to see an organization in which all employees are free and profits are high"—to the overly particular—"I see an organization with yellow drapes." A facilitator takes all the vision statements of the participants and helps the group weave them into an overall vision with a set of goals and objectives for getting there. It is presumed that if the goals are met, the vision will become reality. When you think about it, though, this is very unlikely to happen. It's too rational. It doesn't take account of the messiness of reality and the systemic nature of most complex undertakings. Also, visions arrived at in this way are often more disappointing than inspiring.

It seems as if a vision has the power to inspire only when no one knows exactly how to achieve it. When John Kennedy said we would go to the moon, no one knew exactly how we would do it, including the President. That element of not-knowing-how appears necessary for engaging people's imaginations. Imagination, after all, has much in common with visioning, in that it involves "forming a mental concept of what is not actually present to the senses" and "the mental consideration of actions or events not yet in existence." Our imaginations are the wellsprings of the creativity (another word with roots in the supernatural) that will be necessary for figuring out how to achieve an inspiring vision. Perhaps a vision is inspiring only when it requires imagination and creativity. Perhaps a visionary leader is just an imaginative, creative person. We are drawn to her because she appeals to our imaginations, our creative instincts. Why would we follow anyone who does not?

Visionaries often see across boundaries, such as time or space or paradigms or disciplines or domains that seem discrete to the rest of us. They imagine possibilities where we see impossibilities. They consider things likely that we consider unlikely. As the expression goes, they "think out of the box." This seems more remarkable to us than it does to them, and more notable in retrospect than it seemed when the visioner was cranking away at his idea, day after day. Most visionaries I know think they are talking common sense, given their experiences and interests. Anyone who has read what the visionary has read and seen what the visionary has seen might reasonably conclude what the visionary concluded. Any mechanic who plugs away at engines in the same intellectual context as the Wright Brothers will not think of himself as a "flight visionary." He's just an ordinary person solving one problem after another until his tinker toy soars off, which is what he knew it would do from the beginning, if he just set his mind to it and followed the right steps.

Because few of us share the context within which the visionary is thinking, we have to take his vision largely on faith. Over time, perhaps he will explain enough and we will experience enough so that we see what he sees and why he is confident it can be realized. But for a while, at least, we need to believe because he believes. Visions are for the hopeful, for people who are open to possibilities and like to solve problems. They are not for the skeptical, the "realistic," or the cynical. Visions and visionaries require an uncommon amount of trust. The end state of a vision is usually both clear and unclear (the moon, but where on the moon? a school, but where and what kind?); the process for achieving it is usually wide open; the virtues necessary to discover and manage the process are usually present only as potentialities in people who do not necessarily feel them yet; the amount of work involved is indeterminable. The visionary leader reminds people of the goal, but keeps the vision general enough so they can imagine it in their own terms. He articulates general ideas about the process of getting there, but he has to leave the details to their imaginations and their particular sets of skills. He tells them what virtues will be required—patience, courage, steadfastness, and so on—and he creates opportunities for people to practice and celebrate those virtues. He calls upon followers to find and unleash hitherto untapped powers within themselves. And he affirms progress: We're getting there, look how far we've come, you're doing great work, we're going to make it.

Meanwhile, he does not know exactly what the vision "looks like," has to work with whoever shows up, has to shift ground whenever necessary and take advantage of unforeseen opportunities. Communication between leader and followers is always problematic. I found it impossible to communicate satisfactorily. First of all, if you haven't seen the kind of school I was envisioning, it is hard to envision it. The model of schooling that has been burnt into our minds by 12 years of elementary and secondary education dominates our imaginations. It is hard to think of any way of doing things other than the way we are accustomed to doing them. Moreover, many people can buy into the idea that students should have more say in their learning, but when they see what that looks like in its early stages, they can be appalled. A classroom abuzz with self-directed, independent, curious learners can appear chaotic when compared with a classroom of quiet, compliant students doing seatwork. The leader may know what his words ultimately will entail; his followers may not. The leader may have one vision in mind, but, because he has kept it vague enough to enlist other people's imaginations, some followers may turn out to have something else in mind and can be disillusioned. They will feel they have been misled, that the leader did not communicate well or fully with them.

Most of us have the notions in our heads that everything important can and should be communicated, that if everything is communicated no one will misunderstand anything and everything will go as planned. Again and again, in organization after organization, when things don't go well, the problem is "a failure to communicate." These notions are unsupportable. Everything cannot be communicated, especially where visions are concerned. By definition, they are "not present to the senses," if not mystical or supernatural revelations. They are certainly not in the here and now. Words are insufficient. They can accomplish only what words can accomplish and they can always be misunderstood or misinterpreted. Since only some things, not everything, can be communicated, the most the leader can do is communicate *some* things, and they may not be, to some people, or upon reflection, the *right* things to have communicated. Hindsight is, as they say, twenty-twenty.

Nor should everything be communicated, even if it could be. A leader spends time doing many things. How much of that time should she spend taking action and conversing, documenting her actions and conversations for others, or reflecting upon her actions and conversations so that she can communicate thoughtfully? The answer will always be a compromise, so the leader will always be open to the charge that she did not communicate something that turns out to be important later on. Charismatic leaders may be felt to mislead because they charmed their followers; visionary leaders may be felt to mislead because so much of their vision, and the process of achieving it, is unknown, even to them. Either kind of leader can mislead, simply because there is not world enough and time to communicate all that someone might want communicated or want, in retrospect, to have had communicated.

The most commonly proposed solution to communication problems is more communication, preferably written. Bureaucracies are notorious for requiring written documentation and multiple sign-offs for everything; they're also famous for terrible communication and paralysis brought on by overdocumentation. Without trust, faith, and a tolerance for ambiguity, all is lost. As soon as the visionary leader starts trying to communicate like a bureaucrat, he is a bureaucrat and you can kiss the vision goodbye. What's required is a form of communication that is far more robust than the rational documentation usually meant by people who want more or better communication. Storytelling, for instance, can convey more information per unit of time than rational documentation, and it can build and deepen relationships at the same time. The closer the relationships, the more trust there is. The more trust there is, the better the teamwork and collaboration, the more significant the action that takes place, and the less need for extraneous documentation.

Visionaries are often good storytellers, if only for the obvious reason that a vision is a kind of story. Visions require a willing suspension of disbelief, a familiar plot, and familiar characters. The plot is usually some version of the Promised Land story or the City on a Hill or the Good Society. It's a story of people wanting something better for themselves and their children. They face apparently insurmountable obstacles. When they express their hopes, realists and cynics deride them, but they persist. Their faith is tested. From time to time, they doubt themselves and mistrust their leader and make almost fatal mistakes. But they prevail. Sometimes they prevail through supernatural intervention, usually they prevail through their own sweat and tears, and often they can't tell the difference between the fruits of their labors and divine beneficence. But they achieve their vision, against the odds.

The characters in the drama are so familiar that many of us instinctively play their parts. Each major character represents a virtue necessary for enabling the group to succeed: steadfastness, courage, forthrightness, fidelity, faith, hope, and charity, for instance. As the group moves toward its vision, other virtues and their corresponding vices are enacted and woven into the storyteller/visionary's evolving tale: the adaptable fellow versus the rigid man; the cautious woman versus the rash young girl; the thrifty worker versus the wastrel. At significant opportunities, the leader tells the constantly updated story and rewards the heroes who exemplify the virtues necessary for success. Negative characters and vices are integral, but they must be dealt with as they are in good stories.

Stories are superior forms of communication because they can embed moral instruction as they convey complex information, entertain, appeal to many senses, and deepen relationships. They are normative. Through sharing stories, people involved in pursuing a vision discover, temper, and balance their common values. Subtly, they establish the boundaries within which they are going to work and the rules by which they will regulate themselves. Through stories, leadership becomes a moral enterprise.

Morals concern how human beings treat one another. Some people believe that moral laws come directly and exclusively from sacred texts—the Ten Commandments, for instance. We treat each other in certain ways because our gods exhort us to and may punish us, if we do not. Some believe that morals are practical rules for living, derived not from gods but from thousands of years of experience. Thomas Jefferson thought that each of us is born with the innate moral sense necessary for so social an animal. John Dewey thought that moral sense was an innate social possession, not an individual one. Whether it is sacred or secular, innate or learned; whether the moral sense derives from our emotions or from our reason, it is a central ingredient in everything we do together and it dyes leadership with its colors. All leadership is moral leadership. To the extent that leaders ask for tolerance or fairness or compassion or honesty; to the extent that they appeal to a sense of duty or the rightness of their cause or the need to subordinate one's self-interest to the group's larger interest—leaders are making, and asking for, moral commitments. Leadership is about *judgment*, day in and day out. Our desire to judge leaders back is perfectly understandable, even if we tend to judge them more harshly than ourselves.

5

How does a leader stop leading? When should you drop back and follow, like a bicycle racer? How do you know when it's time for you to go and someone else to take over?

These questions are of considerable interest to business and social entrepreneurs and to founders in every field. When you start something, you want it to outlast you. Moreover, since it is often the case that people who are good at starting something are not necessarily good at sustaining it or leading it through its more mature stages, leadership must change hands for the good of the organization. This can happen with a little or a lot of organizational and personal angst, depending on how the organization or movement has planned its evolution and how the leader has prepared himself or herself psychologically.

When I took one of those Myers–Briggs-type tests that describes your approach to work and your cognitive style, the resulting descriptor of me was "natural leader, cannot not lead." Although I know very well that I can "not lead" and often choose not to lead, there is truth in the characterization. When I get involved in something, I tend to get deeply involved. Others usually look to me for some kind of leadership and I usually oblige. I like most of the aspects of leading, probably because I like people and I like to show that they—and I—can do things that others might not think we can do (tell me it's impossible and I'll start thinking of ways to do it). When I started P.S. 1, however, I put a time limit on my leadership. I said I would lead the school until its charter was renewed—5 years—and then pass the baton. The school could not be considered a success until it had succeeded its founding students, parents, and leaders.

That was easy to say, but hard to do, for many reasons. One reason is that schools are very fluid organizations. By design, students and parents are there for only a few years before graduating or moving on. By circumstance, teachers come and go, as well, especially if you tend to hire young ones, which most charter schools do. It is difficult to build a culture and an identity when so many key people are coming and going and the school is growing by leaps and bounds. Where does the continuity come from? It came from me and from a steadily dwindling group of founding parents and teachers. As we got closer to the time when we had to move on, we found ourselves the sole keepers of the school's history, culture, and values, the only sources of continuity, and the best spokespersons for the enterprise. If we were no longer important for doing the things necessary to start up the business, we were now important for these new roles. When you are still needed, it is hard to leave or even make plans for leaving.

Another reason it is hard to leave is that you never seem to find that situation in which things you started are neatly wrapped up. There always seems to be so much to do, your vision tends to keep sliding into the future so that you do not feel any closer to it, and your standards about how well things must be done before you leave keep rising. Then there are the relationships you have made with students, parents, and teachers, and the commitments you have made, and your love of the job, and the opportunities that seem always just around the corner.

Nevertheless, the summer after our third year, I brought in a business consultant, Bob Beale, to analyze our situation and help us think about how we would move into the next, presumably more mature, phase of our organizational life. The school still needed my leadership because the conditions within which it operated continued to be politically and financially perilous and I was good at dealing with peril. But we wanted to pave the way for a smooth transition to new leadership 2 years hence and wanted to begin grooming future leaders among our students, teachers, and parents. In addition, we wanted everyone, including myself, to be doing only those things that we were good at. We wanted the right people in the right jobs.

At the time, I was the school's executive director, principal, and fund raiser, I taught English part time, and I managed the design and construction of a new building. I shoveled the walks when I couldn't get a student to do it, plunged the toilets, vacuumed, cleaned, picked up, ragged on subcontractors to finish their work, chased kids down the street, and answered any phone that rang more than twice. Linda Reilly, a founding parent, had been overseeing the budget, organizing the parents, connecting teachers to city resources, teaching, and backing me up in both the important tasks and the trivial ones. We were the Mom and Pop of P.S. 1, and everyone came to us for everything. Clearly, we could not do everything that needed doing and clearly we were the wrong people for some of the jobs we were doing. Someone else could do them better than we could, with more enjoyment and less stress. We had experimented with the philosophy that "everyone is responsible for everything" for 3 years, and the staff wanted more specification of duties. They argued that when everyone is responsible for everything, no one is responsible for anything in particular.

As a result of Bob's analysis, we began to restructure the organization, creating some new administrative positions and laying the groundwork for my eventual exit. It was the sensible thing to do, the inevitable thing to do. Whether I would have done it as planned, however, I will never know. In February, a few days after my fifty-seventh birthday, I had a surprise quintuple bypass operation.

The last words I heard before conking out were spoken by the anesthesiologist I had just met: "This will be a profound insult to your narcissism," she said. Truer words were never spoken. Although I knew, intellectually, that I would die one day, I awoke *knowing in my heart* that I would die and that it would be sooner, rather than later. This inevitable discovery may be commonplace, but it knocks everyone who makes it for a loop, nonetheless. You question everything you are doing and every plan you have made. You question who you are, what you have accomplished, and what you can or should do in the precious few moments of life left to you. You are clearly not who you thought you were. You are determined to change your ways.

As I wandered around the house mulling these things over, I grew increasingly depressed. Meanwhile, back at school, people stepped up to the plate and did what needed doing. The school functioned smoothly, day after day, without me. I began to have meetings with key people at my house after a couple of weeks, but I stayed out of the office for 6 weeks and did not work my usual hours when I went in. Things appeared "back to normal" after 10 weeks, but they really weren't. I was different and my colleagues were different. They all saw that their founder and leader could leave them imminently and it would be up to them to carry on. As I confronted my mortality, they confronted the mortality of their jobs and of the organization. They saw, as I did, that I was more fragile than any of us had imagined. Although I kept up my usual banter and played my usual roles, it was clear to most that I was shaken and depressed. The old Rex, who had led them through the fire and over the ramparts and shouted, "We're getting there!" when all they saw was smoke and chaos, was gone. I was weak and uncertain and more interested in saving my life than theirs. My narcissism had indeed been insulted, as the anesthesiologist promised, and I was having trouble getting over it.

I learned a number of things about leadership during my recovery and the ensuing 15 months it took me to leave. The first lesson was how much energy it takes to lead. A week after my operation, a friend and board member came to visit me at home. Although the visit lasted only 15 minutes, I was totally exhausted when she left, and had to go to bed. I had discovered, in the days following the operation, the zero point of personality, the point at which you have no desire and no energy to communicate with anyone about anything. During those 15 minutes I had to rise from the zero point to converse, and after those 15 minutes I fell back to it. I became aware of what it takes, physically and psychologically, *just to have a basic personality*, just to listen to what another person is saying, process it, and think of something to say in response. In the ensuing weeks, I monitored my energy output for different kinds of interactions with people, and eventually I developed a scale. Starting from the zero point, basic, minimal personality requires an output of 100. Interactions involving some frustrations and complexities—a half-hour conversation with a couple of people about a common problem, for instance—require outputs in the 500–700 range. Participation in meetings that involve hard thought, argument, and touchy issues requires outputs in the 1,000–1,500 range. Leadership of such meetings—attending to what is being said, thinking about all the conflicting points of view, weaving in your own point of view, looking for patterns and syntheses, monitoring the meeting's progress as a meeting, thinking about how what is being said fits into larger schemes, value structures, and boundaries, trying to factor in the different personality styles and learning styles, trying to translate, trying to calm this person down and bring out that person who has been silent, shifting roles and perspectives—requires outputs in the 2,500–4,000 range. Speeches, really controversial meetings, high-stress tap dancing routines for funders, and other miscellaneous leadership tasks can require two to three times that output. Having discovered zero, I could see what kind of energy I had become accustomed to spending, I could see that it was an *enormous* amount, and I knew that even if I still did have that kind of energy (which I doubted for a year), I did not want to expend it that way anymore. I needed to conserve it.

I became aware of other components of my leadership when I saw that they were gone after my surgery. For example, I had been—if not *obsessed*—then at least *intensely focused* on the organization for years. P.S. 1 consumed all my waking and much of my dreaming life. It was all I thought about. It was all I did. I gave it everything I had. I think successful leadership often requires that, especially in the early years of an enterprise. After the operation, I was unwilling and unable to focus like that. Before the operation, I was *fearless* and I took enormous risks. After the operation, I was not fearless and I was unwilling to take those kinds of risks. Before the operation, I was supremely confident. Things had gone our way for years and I knew they would continue to. After the operation, I lost that confidence.

I still had the responsibilities of leadership, still felt obligated to meet commitments I had made, still saw that people were looking to me for leadership. But my intensity was gone, my focus was gone, my fearlessness was gone, and my confidence was gone. I even felt that I was slightly less agile, mentally. I could still articulate the vision, but vision alone is not enough, ideas alone are not enough, history and momentum are not enough. Leadership requires enormous energy, something close to obsession, fearlessness, and supreme confidence. When I lost them, I lost the right to lead.

Why is it so hard to "unlead"? It is hard because, say what they will, many followers will not let you stop leading. They will defer to you again and again. They are in the habit of depending on you and you are in the habit of wanting them to depend on you. It is hard because, say what you will, your pride will not let you stop leading. You have invested everything in an enterprise, it is identified with you, and you have identified with it. How can you leave it, especially if it is not perfect yet? Where else will you ever feel so central, so needed and appreciated? You have created a job that exactly matches your interests and talents. You have created problems that only you can fix. Where will you ever find that kind of satisfaction again? It is hard to unlead because you are addicted to your own adrenaline and you don't know what you would do if your life were not always in crisis. It is hard to unlead because it feels like giving up or wimping out. It is as hard to leave your institution as it is to leave your child, even though you know in both cases that you must, for your sake and theirs.

In the end, every leader must know that his or her leadership will not last. Others will replace you and change what you have done. Do not hang around too long. Go do something else. The greatest satisfactions of leadership lie in the process itself and the million-and-one human interactions that are beyond summary and beyond any telling. If you loved the dreaming and the hoping and the problem solving and the uncertainty of it all; if you loved the surprises and mysterious synergies and inexplicable insights and breakthroughs; and if you loved the excitement of people discovering heretofore unknown gifts and thinking together in solidarity and relishing little victories over ignorance and fear—then that should be satisfaction enough.

6

As I see it, the main job of a leader is to *create contexts* within which people can find meaning, direction, and, perhaps, even joy. When you create contexts, you are not directly making things happen. You are defining the possibilities within which a wide, but not infinite, range of things *might* happen, each of which would be congruent with the others and all of which would add up to a coherent movement or condition. As a leader, I didn't "make" people do anything; I made *opportunities* for people to act on shared values and accomplish things they otherwise would not have been able to accomplish.

The word *context* means a "weaving together," an intertwining. What leaders weave most of all is a warp and a woof of people and ideas. In any organization, but especially in an urban high school, the leader's job is to weave relationships. In order to maximize learning throughout the school, you need to create and deepen student-to-student relationships, student–teacher relationships, teacher–teacher relationships, teacher–parent relationships, and school-to-community relationships. Breakdowns in any of them reduce the richness of learning opportunities and slow down the flow of knowledge and information.

What are the contexts within which student-to-student relationships will be positive and fruitful, especially in a school with ethnic and socioeconomic diversity? You need common goals, processes that force frequent and intense interaction, and structures that promote teamwork. Informal sports teams, academic teams, collaborative learning opportunities, entrepreneurial activities, and clubs of all kinds help create the interdependencies that bring students together and deepen their mutual understanding, if not their mutual trust. Whenever possible, it is best if these are conceived and carried out by students, not adults. The only adults involved in student activities should be there by invitation of the students. Grown-ups cannot create a culture for teenagers. They can only create conditions under which teenagers will develop their own natural cultures, and they can do a certain amount of training in things like conflict resolution or mediation or management. This means that students often will create poorly led, disorganized, evanescent, unsuccessful, wrongheaded, or obnoxious clubs, movements, or activities. They may raise uncomfortable questions about the school, adult authority, or standard operating procedure. They will display more enthusiasm than knowledge, more energy than insight, more idealism than realism. Tough. If you want students to learn how to deepen, and take responsibility for, personal and civic relationships, you have to give them the opportunities to do so, and giving people opportunities always entails giving them opportunities to do something badly as well as to do it well. You will be surprised, however, at how often student-generated activities turn out well.

Weaving relationships among students and teachers is difficult. Many urban students have moved around so much that they do not relate well to any adults; many come from families that are "institutionally suspicious"; many are wary of people outside their ethnic group; many nurse negative memories about past treatment by teachers; many are behind, academically, and are extremely self-conscious about their lack of skills and knowledge; many are outright anti-academic. Many teachers in urban schools are insufficiently adept at relating to students who don't like or understand them; many teachers do not know how to individualize instruction; many ask too much or too little of their students; some are not much more socially mature than teenagers. As authority figures in positions of power, teachers are natural targets of teenage ridicule and wrath. Teachers complain that students do not respect them; students echo the sentiment. In the worst schools, no one gets any respect and everyone seems to be daring everyone else to "dis" them. Arguments and fights centering on disrespect of one kind or another consume enormous amounts of time and energy.

Teachers all over the country will tell you that young people today have less respect for their elders than ever before. I don't know if that is true. Civility in general does seem rarer than it used to be. I suspect it is the case that more students today *show* less respect for teachers and their power than they did in my day, and I suspect that more teachers fear students and their power to ruin a class, a day, or a career. Their potential relationships are constrained from the outset by structural arrangements: Students are compelled by law to be in school, whether they want to be there or not; they have had no say in how their school is organized and what it tells them to do; they have no role in decision making or governance; much of what they are forced to study is boring and pointless; and they have fewer rights than the adults in the building—all of this at a time in their lives when they are *keenly* aware of inequities and want *desperately* to escape what they see as parental and social oppression. When you look at schooling from their point of view, it is a wonder that teenagers haven't long since revolted, reduced the schools to rubble, and driven all the teachers and administrators from the land.

The challenge for teachers is to reach across this divide without surrendering their most powerful assets—that they are adults, which all teenagers want to become; and that they know things and can do things that teenagers want to know and do. Students tend to respect people who are passionate about something and very good at it. They willingly will suppress their natural resistance to authority and apprentice themselves to anyone who displays passion and excellence, AND knows them well enough to connect their interests to the subject about which he or she is an authority. Teachers should be authori*tative*, not authori*tarian*. It follows that the best things a school leader can do to cultivate healthy relationships between students and teachers is to help the teachers become authoritative in their fields, help them find ways to know their students' strengths and weaknesses well, and help them learn how to connect student interests to the subject at hand. It helps, too, if the leader can eliminate or mitigate the structural irritants that pit teachers and students against one another even when neither of them wants an adversarial relationship. Students *can* have more say in the organization and governance of the school. They *can* have more say in the curriculum, the pace at which they study various subjects, the ways in which they learn, and where they learn. Students *can* do some of the teaching and teachers *can* do some of the learning. The more that everyone in the building sees himself or herself as a learner, the greater the role that authoritativeness plays in all their lives and the more they consult one another. The result is deeper relationships, based on respect, expertise, and common interests.

Leaders also can raise questions about the disrespect issue and the culture of victimhood that lies behind it. They have to say something like this: "Look, I know that there are real victims in life, I know that there are injustices and inequities and that some of us are in great pain because we have not been treated well or fairly. I know, too, that these histories cannot and should not be swept under the rug or prettied up, this pain and the anger it generates cannot be wished away or ignored. Like you, I feel a natural obligation to help others who are in pain if I can possibly do so. What is necessary for us to help each other in this regard is, first and foremost, a commitment to *not get stuck in the role of victim.* When we get stuck there, when we *identify ourselves as victims,* we are choosing to remain victims, to remain in pain and live in anger. This is a self-destructive choice. This way of being, this kind of energy, does not, cannot, make us or those around us happier or healthier. Blind acting out of rage does not and cannot solve problems that lead to victimization in the first place. In this organization, in this community, you can express your hurt and anger, but you cannot *just* express your hurt and anger. We are going to hold you, and you are going to hold me, to a higher standard, for our own good as individuals and for the good of the group. We are going to *learn* from our feelings. We are going to *grow* and *change,* even *transform* ourselves, using reason and knowledge and certain kinds of conversations that have been shown to contribute to growth and change and health. That's what we do here, whether or not anyone else in the world does it. We are a school. We learn."

It is the leader's job to shape the discourse with comments like this, to influence what people say to one another, when they say it, and how they say it. I don't know how many meetings teachers and students and parents should have—some say fewer and shorter, some say more and longer—but I do know that whenever there are meetings, the discourse, the conversation, should be the kind that deepens understanding, strengthens relationships, and employs the rhetorical tools necessary for learning. This rules out some forms of speech, certain kinds of monologues, and various types of expressive discourse known to destroy trust, flexibility, curiosity, and hope. A leader has to know the difference and make that difference clear to everyone else. We live in an age of emotivism, a time when a great many people believe that the most important component of our humanity is our emotions and the most significant acts we can undertake are acts of expression, sharing, and venting. If such a widespread belief is not evidence of a failed school system, I don't know what is. Educational leaders cannot be emotivists.

Deepening relationships among teachers is easier than building student-to-teacher relationships, but it, too, requires transcending structural constraints that keep teachers isolated from one another. The physical organization of the school building is the most obvious constraint. Add to physical isolation a master schedule that leaves little time for collaborating with colleagues, a professional development schedule that offers but a handful of meetings a year, staff meetings that are as infrequent as they are short and unsubstantive, divergences in professional philosophy, content-area differences, personality clashes, and pecking orders, and the challenge is great indeed. As with creating contexts for all other relationships, creating contexts within which teachers will talk more about their craft and about the quality of student work, requires paying attention to their discourse. Presuming you can restructure the environment and working conditions so that there is more teacher talk, you have to help everyone realize that some conversations are more productive than others. When we were doing the school visits that led to my book *Schools of Thought* (1991), we found that if you go to the teachers' lounge and it is full of cigarette smoke and everyone is griping about students and their families, you might as well leave the school right away; you're not going to see much genuine learning or exciting teaching going on. The most important kinds of teacher talk are those that deepen understanding of the nature, purpose, and quality of teachers' and students' work. The most important modes of teacher talk are those that employ a language of learning—that is, a discourse laced with questions, multiple points of view, empathy, critical and creative thinking, authoritative opinion, and scholarly curiosity. In many schools, this language has been driven to the margins by a discourse of declaration, administration, compliance, command, and control, on the one hand, and a discourse of whining, on the other hand. A leader's first job is to reverse the situation by bringing a language of learning to the forefront and driving "adminispeak" and whining to the margins.

Leadership is about creating contexts; creating contexts is about weaving certain kinds of relationships; weaving the right relationships is about using language in new ways for new ends. It is the special talent of the leader to sense, through listening carefully to what people are saying, what context for action already exists and what alterations to it would bring about different actions. In the final analysis, this sensitivity to the spoken and unspoken words of people in critical relationships is what is decisive. Context is all. My grandmother used to say that certain people "couldn't see the forest for the trees." Leaders *can* see the forest, can see the larger contexts for action that those of us who are caught up in the contexts cannot see. More accurately, they can *hear* what others cannot hear in the conversations that matter. They can tell from the sound of things when there is a gathering of positive energies, and they know what to say that will increase the odds that these positive energies will coalesce into positive experiences, events, and products. What they're listening for are messages that rise above the actual words being exchanged to say something like this: "Here is a good way to go; here is a better way to go; here is what I have learned that is worth passing on."

References

Bellah, R., Madsen, R., Sullivan, W. M., Swidler, A., & Tipton, S. M. (1985). *Habits of the heart: Individualism and commitment in American life.* Berkeley: University of California Press.

Berliner, D. C. (1979). *Tempus educare.* In P. L. Peterson & H. J. Walberg, (Eds.), *Research on teaching* (pp. 120–136). Berkeley: McCutchan

Brown, R. (1991). *Schools of thought: How the politics of literacy shape thinking in the classroom.* San Francisco: Jossey-Bass.

Carnegie Council on Adolescent Development. (1992). *A matter of time: Risk and opportunity in the nonschool hours.* New York: Carnegie Corporation of New York.

Chambers, J., Parrish, T., & Lieberman, J. (2001). *What are we spending on Special Education in the U.S.?* Palo Alto, CA: Center for Special Education Finance, American Institutes for Research, John C. Flanagan Research Center.

Clark, R. M. (1988). *Critical factors in why disadvantaged students succeed or fail in school.* New York: Academy for Educational Development.

deLone, R. (1979). *Small futures: Children, inequality and the limits of liberal reform.* New York: Harcourt Brace Jovanovich.

Finn, C., Jr., Rotherham, A., & Hokanson, C., Jr. (Eds.). (2001). *Rethinking special education for a new century.* Washington, DC: Thomas B. Fordham Foundation and Progressive Policy Institute.

Hallowell, E. (1994). *Driven to distraction.* New York: Simon & Schuster.

Horn, W., & Tynan, D. (2001). Time to make special education special again," in C. Finn, Jr., A. Rotherham, & C. Hokanson, Jr. (Eds.), *Rethinking special education for a new century.*(pp. 23–51). Washington, DC: Thomas B. Fordham Foundation and Progressive Policy Institute.

Howard, P. (1994). *The death of common sense: How law is suffocating America.* New York: Random House.

Kakalik, J. S., Furry, W. S., Thomas, M. A., & Carney, M. F. (1981). *The cost of special education.* Santa Monica, CA: Rand.

Kemmerer, F. (1978–1979). The allocation of student time. *Administrator's Notebook, 2(8).*

Klingner, J. K., Vaughn, S. R., Schumm, J. S., Hughes, M., & Elbaum, B. (1997). Outcomes for students with and without learning disabilities in inclusive classrooms. *Learning Disabilities Research and Practice, 13*, 153–161.

Lyon, G. R., Fletcher, J. M., Shaywitz, S. E., Shaywitz, B. A., Torgesen, J. K., Wood, F. B., Schulte, A., & Olson, R. (2001). "Rethinking learning disabilities," in C. Finn, Jr., A. Rotherham, & C. Hokanson, Jr. (Eds.), *Rethinking special education for a new century* (pp. 259–287). Washington, DC: Thomas B. Fordham Foundation and Progressive Policy Institute.

Mars-Proietti, L. (Ed.). (2002). *The complete learning disabilities directory*. Millerton, NY: Grey House.

Marzano, R. J., Kendall, J. S., & Cicchinelli, L. F. (1998). *What Americans believe students should know: A survey of U.S. adults*. Aurora, CO: Mid-continent Regional Educational Laboratory.

McKnight, J. (1989, Summer). Do no harm: Policy options that meet human needs. *Social Policy*, p. 9.

McKnight, J. (1995). *The careless society: Community and its counterfeits*. New York: Basic Books.

Morgan, G. (1986). *Images of organization*. Newbury Park, CA: Sage.

Perkins, D. (1992). Smart schools: From training memories to educating minds. New York: Free Press.

Purnell, S., & Hill, P. (1992). *Time for reform*. Santa Monica, CA: Rand.

Rosenshine, B. (1980). How time is spent in elementary school classrooms. In C. Denham & A. Lieberman (Eds.), *Time to learn* (pp. 107–126). Washington, DC: U.S. Department of Education.

Smith, B. (2000, December). Quantity matters: Annual instructional time in an urban school system. *Educational Administration Quarterly, 36*(5), 652–682.

Snow, J., & Green, M. (1994). *What's really worth doing and how to do it*. Toronto: Inclusion Press.

Tinder, G. (1980). *Community: Reflections on a tragic ideal*. Baton Rouge: Louisiana State University Press.

Torgesen, J. K., Alexander, A.W., Wagner, R. K., Rashotte, C. A., Voeller, K., Conway, T., & Rose, E. (2001). Intensive remedial instruction for children with severe reading disabilities: Immediate and long-term outcomes from two instructional approaches. *Journal of Learning Disabilities, 34*, 33–58.

Walberg, H. (1988, March). Synthesis of research on time and learning. *Educational Leadership*, pp. 76–85.

Index

About the Author

Rexford G. Brown is a former education policy analyst, education researcher, teacher, and principal. In 1994, after 23 years at The Education Commission of the States, he left his position as Senior Fellow to become Founding Executive Director of P.S. 1, an inner-city middle school/high school in Denver, Colorado. He retired in 2001 to pursue new projects. Brown is the author of *Schools of Thought: How the Politics of Literacy Shape Thinking in the Classroom* (1991), and dozens of articles and reports about schooling in America. He is currently a consultant to leaders of small high schools, and a member of several foundation boards. He lives in Denver, Colorado.